CMMI® Distilled

CMMI® Distilled

Third Edition

*A Practical Introduction
to Integrated
Process Improvement*

**Dennis M. Ahern
Aaron Clouse
Richard Turner**

♦♦Addison-Wesley

Upper Saddle River, NJ • Boston • Indianapolis • San Francisco
New York • Toronto • Montreal • London • Munich • Paris
Madrid • Capetown • Sydney • Tokyo • Singapore • Mexico City

Carnegie Mellon
Software Engineering Institute

The SEI Series in Software Engineering

Special permission to reproduce in this book portions of CMU/SEI-2006-TR-008, CMMI for Development, Version 1.2, Copyright 2006 by Carnegie Mellon University, portions of CMU/SEI-2007-TR-017, CMMI for Acquisition, Version 1.2, Copyright 2007 by Carnegie Mellon University, and selected figures from Introduction to CMMI Version 1.2, Copyright 2006 by Carnegie Mellon University, is granted by the Software Engineering Institute.

SEI Figure Credit List appears on page 249.

Library of Congress Cataloging-in-Publication Data

Ahern, Dennis M.
   CMMI distilled : a practical introduction to integrated process improvement /
Dennis M. Ahern, Aaron Clouse, Richard Turner.—3rd ed.
     p. cm.
   Includes bibliographical references and index.
   ISBN 978-0-321-46108-7 (pbk. : alk. paper)
   1. Capability maturity model (Computer software) I. Clouse, Aaron. II. Turner,
Richard, 1954– III. Title.

QA76.758.A397 2008
005.1068′5—dc22   2008008198

ISBN-13: 978-0-321-46108-7
ISBN-10:   0-321-46108-8
Text printed in the United States on recycled paper at Courier in Stoughton, Massachusetts.
First printing, April 2008

Contents

List of Figures

Preface

CMMI Distilled was originally conceived as a way to introduce the CMMI Product Suite and model-based continuous process improvement to a wide audience. Our goal was to offer a succinct, no-nonsense, minimal-jargon, wittily written, practical guide that was less than half the weight of the "official" CMMI book. We wanted to describe the origins of the model and give the readers some insight into how the 200-plus CMMI authors worked (and fought) to produce it. The first edition had a good deal of "why" information, aimed at folks who had used one of the three source models and who wanted to understand how CMMI differed from earlier models. Of course, it also had the "what" and "how" information about CMMI Version 1.0.

The second edition coincided (roughly) with the release of CMMI Version 1.1, so it included significant changes to the original "what" and "how" sections. At that point CMMI was no longer new and people were beginning to move away from the source models, so we removed some of the "why" material. To reflect the broader reach of CMMI and the need to support practitioners in acquiring sponsors for their improvement initiatives, the second edition added material aimed at managers rather than practitioners.

CMMI content and usage continue to evolve, so now we have created a third edition, building on the legacy of the first two. CMMI began as a tool for managing improvements in engineering development organizations, with a focus on systems and software. In CMMI Version 1.2, this attention to engineering has been strengthened by including explicit hardware-related information. More intriguing, however, are two new members of the CMMI Product Suite: one for the acquirer of systems instead of the developer, and the other for service providers instead of product builders. With these two additions, the potential scope of application for CMMI within an organizational enterprise has broadened significantly. At the same time, CMMI is finding use outside the traditional engineering field. For example, it has been adopted by enterprises as varied as medical facilities seeking to improve their patient care and government entities trying to build and improve their infrastructure.

We had three primary reasons for writing the third edition of *CMMI Distilled.*

1. We wanted to update the book to include changes to the CMMI architecture, content, and presentation, as well as the ongoing domain extensions to the model. The full, updated model content for version 1.2 is covered in the same way as in our previous editions. We use the graphics from the CMMI training material and describe the model components clearly and simply.

2. We wanted to further reduce the amount of historical information relating to the origins of CMMI. For those who may be interested, this material is well covered in the previous editions of this book.

3. We wanted to update and expand upon the practical advice we offer for those using the model. In this edition, we more fully address CMMI usage in tandem with Six Sigma, lean engineering, and other continuous improvement approaches. We also discuss some of the changes to the appraisal methods; specifically, we provide additional guidance on preparing for and managing appraisals, and on using the appraisal results as a powerful input to improvement activities.

Those who have read the previous editions of this book will not be surprised to find that we have included yet another literary offering (three songs) addressing CMMI and the world of continuous improvement. In fact, for those of you who may have missed the first two editions, the earlier "literary gems" can be found on the Pearson Web site at informit.com/aw under either "literary gems" or "superfluous material"—for some reason, the editors were still discussing this as of publication.

And so, in recognition of the explosive growth of CMMI as a process improvement tool of choice around the world, and having incorporated the most recent developments in the evolution of the model suite, we are pleased and excited to present this third edition of *CMMI Distilled.* We hope that it will continue to help our readers understand the CMMI Product Suite and use it wisely for their continuous improvement initiatives.

As always, we couldn't have put this third edition together without the support, wisdom, and patience of our wonderful wives. Pam, Debbi, and Jo—we still love you the best of all!

Dennis, Aaron, and Rich

April 2008

The Tower of Babel
Gustave Dore (1832–1883)

Part I

Integrated Process Improvement

In the biblical story of the Tower of Babel, God caused a construction project to fail by interrupting communication through the creation of multiple languages. In the modern story of process improvement, we have created multiple languages to serve various organizational disciplines through divergent process improvement models and methods. As with the Tower of Babel story, this diversity poses a threat to communication. Capability Maturity Model Integration (CMMI) and integrated process improvement in general strive to reverse this situation by providing a single language through which multiple disciplines can share process improvement activities and a unified focus on process improvement objectives.

Part I Contents

3

Chapter 2. Implementing Continuous Improvement

In which the authors take a wide-ranging look at the tools and methods available to support a culture of continuous improvement that may help readers meet their business objectives.

Chapter 1

Why Integrated Process Improvement?

It is not necessary to change. Survival is not mandatory.
W. Edwards Deming (1900–1993)

The complexity of practice has always dwarfed the simplicity of theory.
Robert Britcher, *The Limits of Software* (1999)

Given that you are reading (or at least browsing through) this book, either you are interested in continuous process improvement and Capability Maturity Model Integration (CMMI), or you have been told to get interested in it. Perhaps your management chain or a major customer has indicated that your organization should be at least CMMI "level 3." You think: "Should I really be interested? Will it make it easier for me to do my job? What is level 3? What is CMMI?" This book will help you answer these questions.

Chapter 1 reviews the business context for any improvement initiative, explaining why that manager or customer may be encouraging you to undertake such an initiative. To understand the rationale for change, it's important to look at some shortcomings of traditional process improvement when faced with the engineering paradigm of the twenty-first century. The engineering world has changed in at least three significant areas since the introduction of model-based process improvement.

First, the environment within which engineering is performed has become increasingly complex. Efforts are larger, involve more people, cross corporate and international boundaries, are distributed far and wide, and must adhere to continually compressing implementation schedules so as to meet customer needs and heightened expectations.

Second, the way in which engineering work is performed has evolved. Cross-discipline teams, concurrent engineering, integration of commercial off-the-shelf (COTS) and open-source software rather than traditional software development, agile and evolutionary development approaches, highly automated processes, and multinational standards are all trends that have affected engineering practice. These changes, in turn, have inspired modifications in the role of the engineering manager.

Third, the continuing proliferation of process improvement models, methods, and standards has increased the challenge of defining and managing process improvement activities. Organizations have adopted multiple approaches to continuous improvement to address their critical processes.

All of these trends highlight the need to integrate process improvement efforts. The myriad disciplines and processes involved in contemporary engineering are closely intertwined. Unfortunately, the overhead and confusion resulting from the application of multiple models and methods are too costly in terms of business expenses and resource allocation. As a consequence, a means of addressing process improvement across a number of disciplines within a single framework is needed. This chapter discusses how changes in the engineering world have influenced the effectiveness of traditional process improvement strategies and explores how organizations can benefit from applying an integrated approach to reach their business objectives.

Model-Based Process Improvement

Model-based process improvement involves the use of a structured framework to guide the improvement of an organization's processes. Process improvement grew out of the quality management work of Deming,[1] Crosby,[2] and Juran[3] and is aimed at increasing the capability of work processes. Essentially, process capability is the inherent ability of a process to produce planned results. As the capability of a process increases, it becomes predictable and measurable, and the most significant causes of poor quality and productivity are controlled or eliminated. By steadily improving its process capability, the organization "matures." Maturity improvement requires strong management support and a consistent long-term focus. In addition, it necessitates fundamental changes in the way managers and practitioners perform their jobs.

One framework for achieving this focus has been the use of a capability model. Models provide a common set of process requirements that capture successful practices and practical knowledge in a format that can be used as a guide in setting priorities. By using a model, organizations can modify or create processes by incorporating practices that have been proven to increase process capability. They may also employ models to conduct an appraisal of process capability for two purposes: to establish a baseline for improvement and to measure progress as improvement activities proceed.

Generally, model-based process improvement begins with management commitment and an appraisal of the organization's existing processes. The findings from this appraisal, in turn, feed action plans. When these plans have been completed, further appraisals are performed and the cycle continues. The goal is for the organization to mature so that it continuously monitors and

(continued)

---

1. Deming, W. Edwards. *Out of the Crisis*. Cambridge, MA: MIT Center for Advanced Engineering, 1986.
2. Crosby, P. B. *Quality Is Free*. New York: McGraw-Hill, 1979.
3. Juran, J. M. *Juran on Planning for Quality*. New York: MacMillan, 1988.

> ### Model-Based Process Improvement (continued)
>
> improves its processes, consistently produces high-quality prod-
> ucts, is agile within its marketplace, and adjusts quickly to cus-
> tomer needs. For a discussion of both model-based and other
> improvement techniques, see the *CMMI Survival Guide* by Garcia
> and Turner.[4]

1.1 Business Objectives and Process Improvement

First, let's talk about your organization and how you or your management might like it to perform. Organizations generally have many different business objectives:

- Produce quality products or services
- Create value for the stockholders
- Be an employer of choice
- Enhance customer satisfaction
- Increase market share
- Implement cost savings and successful practices
- Gain industry-wide recognition for excellence

To achieve a strong competitive edge in a rapidly moving marketplace,
you might like to aggressively take advantage of opportunities and
avoid simply reacting to change. You might also like to improve your
ability to predict costs and revenues, find ways to raise productivity,
and implement means to lower expenses. These measures could help
you to anticipate problems, and develop ways to address them early.

To meet any of these objectives, you must have a clear understanding
of what it takes to produce your products or services. To improve, you
need to understand the variability in the processes that you follow, so
that when you adjust them, you'll know whether the adjustment is

---

4. Garcia, Suzanne, and Richard Turner. *CMMI Survival Guide: Just Enough Process Improvement*,
Boston: Addison-Wesley, 2007.

advantageous. In short, you'll want to manage your business using accurate data about both products and processes.

But wait: How do you know that your data is reasonable or accurate? Can you compare information between projects? Generally, there has to be some consistency in the work you do if you are to make valid comparisons. You want to be able to measure your success and make sure that the processes you follow add value to the products and services that you provide. Of course, that implies a standard way of doing things and a baseline against which to measure your subsequent efforts.

Now we are getting down to the nitty-gritty: Does your organization have experience with writing and following a process, and can it support the development of common, standard processes? Can you determine the best ways to go about a particular task? Establishing standard processes that are appropriate and successful for your workplace and business is fundamental for process control and improvement. Unfortunately, it may not be within the scope of your position descriptions or training. And what about that training?

Without good project management and fundamental technical skills, projects cannot operate effectively enough to spend any time on improvement. Basic activities such as planning and tracking need to be understood and encouraged. Version control and risk management are essential disciplines that need to be addressed. In addition, managing requirements so that you deliver value to your customer is a key business objective.

As you can see from the preceding discussion, getting to the point where your organization enjoys a competitive edge requires a number of incremental improvements. That's where process improvement can really help. Process improvement activities focus on improving process capability, organizational maturity, process efficiency, and process control so as to help you advance the organization and accomplish its objectives. They can provide you with guidance on how to document and standardize processes, increase your work effectiveness, limit rework, measure the performance of the organization, and use the data to manage the business.

Of course, there is a cost associated with process improvement. Experience shows that it can take between 2 percent and 10 percent of normal engineering effort to support a significant process improvement initiative. At the same time, experience also confirms that process improvement brings a significantly positive return on investment (ROI) and improvement in key business indicators. Consider these representative examples of CMMI successes:

- DB Systems GmbH reported that its costs dropped 48 percent from a baseline prior to SW-CMM maturity level 2 as the organization moved toward CMMI maturity level 3.[5]

- As the organization moved from SW-CMM maturity level 3 to CMMI maturity level 5, IBM Australia Application Management Services saw its on-time delivery increase by 10 percent, its on-budget delivery improve by 41 percent, customer satisfaction rise by 33 percent, and application development productivity improve by 76 percent, resulting in a cumulative costs savings of AU$412 million to the company's client.[6]

- Northrop Grumman IT Defense Enterprise Solutions, a CMMI maturity level 5 organization whose engineers had undergone Personal Software Process (PSP) training, reduced identified defects from 6.6 to 2.1 per KLOC over three causal analysis and resolution cycles.[7]

- Reuters' schedule variance decreased from approximately 25 percent to 15 percent as the organization moved from CMM maturity level 3 to CMMI maturity level 5.[8]

As these examples demonstrate, process improvement promises significant benefits for organizations. In the remainder of this chapter, we show how integrating process improvement across several disciplines can increase those benefits.

---

5. Richter, Alfred, "Quality for IT Development and IT Service Operations: CMMI and ITIL in a Common Quality Approach." London: ESEPG, June 16, 2004.

6. Nichols, Robyn, and Colin Connaughton, *Software Process Improvement Journey: IBM Australia Application Management Services. A Report from the Winner of the 2004 Software Process Achievement Award* (CMU/SEI-2005-TR-002). Pittsburgh, PA: Software Engineering Institute, Carnegie Mellon University, 2005.

7. Hollenbach, Craig, "Quantitatively Measured Process Improvements at Northrop Grumman IT." Denver, CO: CMMI User Group and Conference, November 2003.

8. Iredale, Paul, "The 'Internal Offshore' Experience at Reuters." Adelaide, Australia: Australian SEPG, September 27–29, 2004.

Process Improvement and Golf

If you haven't got a handle on what process improvement is and how it can help your business, here's a nonbusiness way to think about it. The process you use to produce a product or service may be likened to a golf swing, in that it is a complex sequence of closely coupled activities that are performed in an integrated manner to achieve a specific purpose. Of course, as we all know, improving your golf swing is not an easy task. Neither is improving your business processes.

First, it's impossible to address all facets of your golf swing at once. You need to break it into pieces so you can concentrate on making adjustments that are under your control. Some of those pieces, such as your grip and your stance (not to mention the club length, the flexibility of the shaft, the material in the club head, and so on), are fundamentals that have to be in place before the reliability of any of the other pieces can be considered. In other words, you have to take care of them before you can make significant progress in other areas.

Second, you can't easily take a critical look at your own golf swing. You need an objective eye (the golf professional or a video camera) that can help evaluate what is right and what isn't. Of course, you also need some measures of correctness to use as a guide in making these determinations.

Third, as you improve the components of the swing (such as grip, stance, length of backswing, and tempo), they begin to merge into a more integrated whole that you can begin to "groove" into predictable consistency. And once you find the swing that's comfortable with your 7 iron, it then needs to be applied (with appropriate adjustment) to the other clubs in your bag.

Finally, it's only after you have achieved consistency in your swing that you can begin to modify it for the situation at hand and really address the strategic parts of golf—club selection, shot placement, draws and fades, and other nuances that most of us see only on television.

In many respects, organizational process improvement works in much the same way as improving your golf swing. Models and

(continued)

> ### Process Improvement and Golf (continued)
>
> other continuous improvement techniques can help you break your process into pieces, show you the fundamentals, and help you decide which aspects to work on first. Process improvement champions, groups, and consultants can help you evaluate your current processes and measure your improvement. The standard processes that you employ can provide you with standard data, which then becomes the basis for your projects to "groove" their activities so that applying them to new areas and thinking strategically become normal ways to work.
>
> And by the way, improving your organization may be easier than improving your golf swing because you have a lot of talent that can work synergistically, and they don't have to do it only on weekends. Go get 'em, Tiger.

1.2 The Engineering Environment of the Twenty-First Century

Remember when there was only one telephone company and only one kind of phone service? When the only telephone-related worry you had was keeping long-distance calls under three minutes? When you understood not only the principles but also (perhaps) the mechanics of how the system worked?[9] Unfortunately (or fortunately in some cases), the era of such relatively simple systems has ended. When you realize that your new telephone contains more software than the lunar landing module, Dorothy's plaintive cry, "Toto, I don't think we're in Kansas anymore," may all too closely echo your feelings of consternation. Even technology-savvy engineers occasionally profess a sense of awe about the relentless pace of technological change. No one can deny that this change has brought new capabilities, new conveniences, and new complexity.

---

9. If you are too young to remember this time, ask a parent or other elder within your circle of friends. They'll appreciate the time to reminisce. If they begin to talk about the value of hard work, the buying power of the dollar, or walking 20 miles to school barefoot in the snow uphill both ways, however, make your escape quickly!

We are now on the rising edge of the system complexity curve, and there is little chance of moderation in the foreseeable future. The U.S. Department of Defense has estimated that it will soon need to field systems utilizing as many as 40 million lines of software code. In some autonomous military systems, software will provide decision-making functions for reconnaissance and weapon delivery.

Many traditionally hardware modules now contain significant microcode that will inevitably interface in some manner with a software control system housed in yet another hardware device. In increasingly complex systems, the ability to differentiate between hardware and software functions may become nearly impossible, complicating design and maintenance tasks and significantly affecting our ability to calculate expected reliability. This complexity is readily evident in the products and systems being conceived, designed, and manufactured each day; moreover, it is mirrored in the activities of the acquiring and developing organizations, both in industry and government. As if the complexity of modern systems was not enough, now more attention is being focused on "systems of systems," as better integration of functions across individual systems is needed.

As systems grow more complex, the processes used to develop them will follow suit. The complexity of processes inevitably increases to keep pace with the number of individuals who are involved in their execution. The theory and concepts of process improvement are elegant and understandable. When we apply them to increasingly complex systems, however, we find that, as Robert Britcher writes, "the complexity of practice has always dwarfed the simplicity of theory."[10] This result is particularly likely when the processes cut across organizational, discipline, corporate, or cultural boundaries.

With large and complex organizations, processes, and systems, process improvement activities can easily become lost in the multiplicity of tasks, agendas, and personalities. Because each office or organization has its own responsibilities and diligently strives to improve its own practices, process improvement efforts can evolve into a patchwork of unrelated and uncoordinated activities spread across a variety of

---

10. Britcher, Robert, *The Limits of Software*. Reading, MA: Addison-Wesley, 1999. This fascinating treatise on the philosophy and practice of software engineering is drawn from the author's work with IBM on the Federal Aviation Administration's (FAA) Advanced Automation System (AAS). AAS was terminated after expenditures of approximately $2 billion, based on the judgment that it could not be accomplished.

organizations. Multiple groups and their executives may vie for limited process improvement resources. Various process groups may select different and sometimes conflicting improvement models. Competition can emerge between groups, and the ownership of process improvement can become hotly debated. In the end, often more energy is spent on the peripheral activities than on the improvement initiatives.

Lest you think that only large organizations have process problems, consider the small, entrepreneurial firm racing to capitalize on a rapidly approaching market window. Such an organization finds it difficult—if not impossible—to address process improvement when the time-to-market criterion is so crucial to its survival. Such a firm often has personnel performing multiple engineering functions simultaneously; conceivably, it may have a different process for each individual in the company. As another example, an information technology application services company may be forced to deal with an erratic customer who constantly changes requirements, priorities, and schedules, leaving little alternative for the firm except to function in a crisis development environment. Although neither type of organization described here has the financial or people resources to pursue traditional process improvement, each could benefit greatly from taking a more disciplined approach to engineering.

1.3 Evolving Engineering Approaches

The organization of engineering and product development work has undergone significant changes in recent years. Much of this change has been aimed at eliminating the inefficiencies associated with stepwise development, in which intermediate work products are handed off to next phase workers, who may have to do significant rework to correct misunderstandings. Concurrent engineering, cross-discipline teams, cross-functional teams, integrated product teams (IPT), and integrated product and process development (IPPD) all represent ways to address this problem and apply the necessary expertise at the appropriate time throughout the product or service life cycle. In practice, this trend means that designers and customers work with manufacturers, testers, and users to support the manufacturing organization in developing requirements. It has also been described as having "everyone at the table," implying that all critical stakeholders support all phases of product or service development.

Understandably, the concept of concurrency has redefined the nature of organizational structure and development. It requires an enhanced management competency for dealing with "gray areas" and ambiguity, which is not easy for many managers who are perhaps more versed in dealing with tangible facts and figures. The general acceptance and rapid deployment of cross-discipline or cross-functional teams in the engineering world has also proved to be a thorny issue for process improvement. The concept of functional departments, each with its own processes under its own control, strongly clashes with the highly interactive work style associated with cross-discipline teams.

To date, discrete process improvement models and techniques have not effectively supported the "mixing bowl" environment of concurrent engineering. If the hardware engineering department is using one approach, the software developers are using a second approach, and the outsourcing and contracts departments are using yet another strategy, problems are inevitable. Separate "stovepipe" models and methods offer little chance of improving the processes used by a cross-discipline team where every member is an actor in most of the processes and the separation between the disciplines has gone the way of the Berlin Wall.

Rather than relying on the strict stages of classical development, cross-discipline teams use integrated processes that are matched more closely to the ebb and flow of the emerging life cycle models and agile development methods They take advantage of evolutionary development approaches and innovative design techniques. Attempting to apply the discipline-specific methods to such processes is analogous to requiring members of a jazz trio to strictly play their individual parts. Of course it's possible—but the outcome is not very satisfying. What is needed is an approach to improvement that not only integrates the disciplines, but also integrates the processes themselves and supports effective work among various stakeholders, functional personnel, and management.

The advent of agile processes and the extension of spiral development to systems and "systems of systems" add an additional twist to the engineering process. These methods challenge much of the traditional industrial approach, replacing it with a more flexible and change-neutral process. There is still a great deal of discussion as to how process improvement is defined and measured in these paradigms, particularly when changes to the process may be as frequent as changes to the product requirements. A good discussion of the impact of agile and spiral approaches may be found in *Balancing Agility and Discipline* by Boehm and Turner.[11]

1.4 A Proliferation of Models and Standards

If imitation is a measure of success, then the Capability Maturity Model for Software (CMM) was exceptionally successful—and for good reason. People in many disciplines were attracted to the elegance of the CMM concept and its close ties to quality management theory and practice. The general response was, "Hey, that's a great idea. Let's build something like that for *our* shop." The end result was a number of similar models that shared intent but not terminology or construction and, therefore, were difficult to use together or to compare results.

At the same time, several international standards have been created that address similar issues:

- ISO/IEC 15288, an international standard on system life cycle processes, was first issued in 2002 and reissued in 2008.[12]
- ISO/IEC 12207, an international standard on software life cycle processes, was first issued in 1995 and amended in 2002 and again in 2004, and reissued in 2008.
- ISO/IEC 15504, an international standard that defines the requirements for performing process assessments that (in various parts), was first issued between 2003 and 2006.

Finally, other approaches to achieving process improvement benefits have been widely implemented. These include Six Sigma and lean engineering and manufacturing.

---

11. Boehm, Barry, and Richard Turner, *Balancing Agility and Discipline: A Guide for the Perplexed.* Boston: Addison-Wesley, 2005.
12. ISO is the International Organization for Standardization; IEC is the International Electrotechnical Commission. For current information on international standards in the areas of systems engineering and software, see http://www.jtc1-sc7.org/.

1.5 The Benefits of Integrated Process Improvement

In the preceding sections, we enumerated many factors that complicate process improvement. It is our assertion that overcoming many of these obstacles is possible by integrated, continuous process improvement. Of course, you may need to be convinced that this endeavor is worthwhile for your organization. At the end of the day, what are the real benefits of integrated process improvement?

Fundamentally, process improvement integration significantly affects four areas: cost, focus, process integration, and flexibility. Some of these changes are more easily quantified than others, but all represent real advantages.

1.5.1 Cost Benefits

Cost containment is probably the easiest benefit to understand. Although integration requires additional investment, the savings from process improvement integration can be significant. By applying a common approach to continuous improvement, organizations can reduce the costs attached to the following endeavors:

- Training in multiple approaches, including models and appraisal methods
- Performing multiple appraisals within the same organizations (and possibly with the same practitioners)
- Maintaining redundant process assets in a repository
- Maintaining or purchasing expertise in multiple approaches

The enhanced probability of success that arises from integrated process improvement also makes it more likely that the organization will achieve cost savings resulting from higher quality, better predictability, and all the other benefits of improved processes.

1.5.2 Clarity of Focus

Within the diverse world of engineering organizations, particularly when projects cut across organizational boundaries, it is difficult to achieve the critical mass necessary to bring about real improvement. This problem can be characterized as a lack of focus and a need to unify the disparate activities. That is, the pressures from outside the group are too strong, the costs too high, or the resources too thinly applied to both improve local processes and interface them with other organizations or disciplines. Budget changes, the business environment, internal politics, and mergers all take their toll by consuming resources that might otherwise be applied to improvement.

An integrated process improvement program can clarify the goals and business objectives of the various constituencies. By integrating process improvement activities across a wider range of disciplines, it becomes easier to rally the troops—both practitioners and executives—to the process improvement banner. Having a single process improvement focus can unify and reinforce vision, efficiently marshal and apply scarce resources, and provide a common language for improvement across various disciplines. In particular, a single model with common terminology and common appraisal methods helps to provide this kind of focus.

A word of caution is appropriate at this point. Not every model can become the focus for continuous process improvement. If the focus doesn't include all of the disciplines critical to organizational success, it will miss the breadth actually needed to improve the organization's operations. An integrated approach allows personnel in each discipline to identify with the processes and feel that they have a stake in the now-focused process improvement program.

1.5.3 Process Integration and Lean Organizations

One of the less obvious benefits of integrated process improvement is the "integrating" effect it has on organizations. When processes are defined across organizational and discipline boundaries, new understanding and mutual education often occur, resulting in the streamlining of the critical work flow and the elimination of redundant or unneeded activities.

Stovepipe[13] process improvement often assumes that interfaces between organizations work effectively; rarely is one process implementer aware of closely related or redundant activities in a sister stovepipe. By working on improving processes across the board, the organization essentially obtains a bonus reengineering effort as a by-product of the process improvement initiative. This streamlining sup-

---

13. Stovepipe processes are usually organized by discipline and do not include the interfaces between those organizations.

ports the lean concept, which strives to provide increased value to the customer by eliminating waste in the production of products.[14]

1.5.4 Agility

A final benefit is the ability to adapt to and exploit business or engineering environment changes. Integrated, continuous process improvement creates and supports an organization that is comfortable with changes associated with refining their work processes. Having a common process infrastructure allows changes to rapidly enter critical work processes, increasing the rate of both infusion and diffusion.[15] Decision making and strategic planning are more efficient and effective given capable processes across disciplines and maturity across organizations. Organizational changes such as corporate reorganizations, mergers, acquisitions, and teaming may be able to benefit from common process language. This benefit may be moot, however, if the organizations involved have chosen radically different process implementations.

1.6 Conclusions

This chapter argued that integrated process improvement can be an effective and efficient way of addressing a wide range of business objectives. It identified changes in the engineering environment, discussed the integration of processes across the product life cycle, and described a cacophony of competing standards—three factors that strongly suggest the need for integrated process improvement. Finally, it defined the benefits of such an approach beyond the simplification of an organization's improvement efforts.

Any change requires letting go of old ways of doing business—even ways that may have been successful to some degree in the past. This can affect not only the way in which those directly involved in projects work, but also the way in which managers at all levels understand their roles. To maximize the chance for true improvement, managers need to lead the effort to make process improvement a way of life across the

---

14. Womack, James P., and Daniel Jones, *Lean Thinking*. New York: Simon and Schuster, 1996.
15. For a discussion of measuring infusion and diffusion, see Garcia and Turner, *CMMI Survival Guide: Just Enough Process Improvement*.

organization, even in the face of the constant need to deal with short-term problems.

Chapter 2 offers some practical advice on taking the plunge and implementing an integrated approach to continuous improvement. By providing some guiding principles for how process improvement integration works in large and small organizations, we hope to ease your implementation of this beneficial approach.

But what if your organization isn't complex or multidisciplinary? Single-model or single-technique process improvement works perfectly well in some organizations. Nevertheless, we invite you to look carefully at the CMMI product suite and its role in an integrated approach to continuous improvement before returning to or beginning your single-model effort. The integration of disciplines in CMMI has produced a better model in a number of ways, even when applied just to a single discipline. Besides, as a result of learning CMMI you'll be a lot better informed if your new CEO starts preaching the benefits of cross-disciplinary teams and a unified approach to continuous improvement.

Chapter 2

Implementing Continuous Improvement

Do what you can, with what you have, where you are.
Theodore Roosevelt (1858–1919)

We find by experience (our own or another's) what is hurtful or helpful.
Giovanni Battista Lamperti, *Vocal Wisdom* (1895)

I have but one lamp by which my feet are guided,
and that is the lamp of experience.
Patrick Henry, Speech before the Virginia Convention (1775)

You learned in Chapter 1 why an integrated approach to process improvement may make sense for both you and your organization. In this chapter, we continue on that path and explore various aspects of an integrated approach. Specifically, we discuss what must be in place for you to think about making ongoing "continuous" improvements in an integrated manner. We address various topics such as tools and methods that are available to you, and the importance of demonstrating leadership and of having a customer and quality focus. We describe "five keys" for continuous improvement (process excellence, CMMI, lean, Six Sigma, and knowledge management) and indicate how they complement each other. We explore ways to manage continuous improvement activities and show how everyone in an organization has a role to play. Finally, we conclude with some pearls of wisdom as take-away thoughts from these first two chapters.

2.1 Driving Business Performance

In many organizations (including yours, one hopes), management focuses on how to stay highly effective and how to make needed improvements. In larger organizations, you might address the need to improve by making the enterprise more integrated. Whether small or large, vital activities for continuous improvement focus on enhancing business performance across the organization. For those efforts to succeed, every employee should be aware of the rationale and goals for improvement. Continuous improvement is a process in which everyone in the organization may be expected (frequently and routinely) to participate and contribute. While major process improvement activities might be conducted by small teams, making processes better is an everyday responsibility for which everyone is accountable.

If you want your organization to succeed both now and in the future, then you need to operate in a well-orchestrated, data-driven, and process-focused manner. Your goal should be to develop and nurture a strong culture of relentless process improvement—a learning environment that is highly responsive to customers, shareholders, and employees. Organizational objectives associated with this learning environment might include these outcomes:

- Establishing a culture of continuous improvement across the organization
- Creating and sustaining a framework to drive business results, measured by financial performance, new-business capture rate, and customer satisfaction
- Identifying, evaluating, promoting, and supporting the deployment of appropriate continuous improvement methodologies, practices, and tools, such as those currently used in (but not limited to) the lean, Six Sigma, theory of constraints, ISO, and CMMI initiatives

- Identifying and sharing successful (and unsuccessful) practices[1] across the organization
- Implementing a robust set of leading indicators that give advanced warning of potential problems
- Being the employer of choice for employees

By realizing these objectives, an organization may improve its financial performance; attract, retain, and fully leverage the talent that it has; and be a trusted provider for its customers.

Chances are good that many of the activities that are included under the banner of "continuous improvement" have been under way in your organization for some time. Supporting policies and procedures may be in place already. Employees who provide outstanding service may be given appropriate recognition and rewards. You may use metrics to manage daily operations. Perhaps your organization invests in providing employees with the training they need to do their jobs, and in developing the leaders who will forge the way in the years ahead. It may be that the lessons learned on one program are used on subsequent programs. All of these are elements of a continuous improvement culture: process discipline, applied learning, employee recognition, collection and use of metrics, training and development, and the identification and deployment of successful practices.

To really drive business performance, however, you may need to leverage your existing efforts. Reevaluating, refocusing, reemphasizing, and communicating the combined effect of those efforts may be a key step in developing and nurturing a strong culture of continuous improvement. Often organizations will reward the heroes who have had the fortitude and wisdom to get the organization out of trouble when programs faltered in meeting their objectives. But what if the organization chose to provide equal rewards to those whose fortitude, wisdom, and leadership keep the organization out of trouble in the first place? What a concept!

---

1. You usually hear about "best practices," right? Rich has spent several years attempting to change that terminology. In his experience, there is no such thing as a "best practice"—only practices that have shown to be useful within a specific context. That same practice could be useless or even detrimental in another context (e.g., an avionics system may benefit from formal verification, whereas a Web site that changes daily would not). Given that we are generally talking about improvement here, a case can be made for improving "good" practices to "better" ones. In any event, the term "best practice" is misleading. We prefer to use "successful" (or "unsuccessful") to describe practices that provide useful knowledge. Unsuccessful processes and practices are as critical to understand as successful processes and practices.

Management needs to make sure that there is a general understanding of its vision for continuous improvement—why it is being pursued and how it may affect employees. The goal should be to sharpen the tools that are used to improve the organization's operations, so that problems are addressed and their solutions enhance the business, and so that data is used to analyze and improve organizational processes. The use of such tools may produce a quantifiable financial gain for the organization. Improvement objectives must also be aligned with customer priorities and with efforts to improve earnings and cash flow. Management should willingly invest in improvement projects, but only when there is a strong business case that such investment is justified. One essential goal (to avoid a frequent need for crisis management) is to uncover the root causes of ongoing problems and to make systemic changes to processes so as to guard against the reoccurrence of those problems. This will free up the wonderful, creative talent in the workforce to focus more on value-added activities. When performance and products are aligned and equally recognized for their excellence by customers, shareholders, and employees alike, an organization will be on the road to becoming a truly world-class operation that is deeply committed to continuous improvement.

A Note for Smaller Organizations

Continuous improvement is not just for the big guys who have loads of overhead available. All of the concepts presented here—including the content of CMMI—are just as valid and appropriate for small and medium-size organizations. If you belong to such an organization, however, you will need to focus even more precisely on the business value of your improvement initiative. One benefit of smaller organizations is that they may have a much easier time selling the idea of continuous change, because there are fewer layers of possibly reluctant stakeholders to convert or satisfy. As you read the remainder of this chapter, think about how each of the elements might affect a smaller business, and note which elements seem to target those specific problem areas with which you have been struggling, or those places where, with improved performance, you might forge ahead of your competition. In *CMMI Survival Guide*, Garcia and Turner provide a wealth of material on improvement for smaller organizations.

2.2 Elements of Continuous Improvement

The key elements of continuous improvement include the following issues:

- Understanding the tools for improvement
- Nurturing a continuous improvement culture
- Providing strong leadership
- Linking improvement to business strategies and results
- Focusing on the customer
- Making quality as important as cost and schedule
- Establishing criteria for larger improvement events

2.2.1 Understanding the Tools for Improvement

Often different parts of an organization (such as engineering, supply-chain management, and manufacturing) are schooled in different tools and approaches for process improvement. Perhaps you work at a site or in a department that has favored one set of methods and techniques over others. As a result, you may not be equally well acquainted with all of your options for continuous improvement. In a smaller organization, you might find that everyone follows only one approach while ignoring others.

One reason for this variation is that many process improvement approaches have their origins in specific and limited areas of the enterprise. For example, lean engineering began in the manufacturing world, as did Six Sigma. In contrast, CMMI was created from the Capability Maturity Model for Software and the Systems Engineering Capability Model—models that addressed two key aspects of the engineering development world. Your goal now should be to apply continuous improvement tools to all aspects of an operation, and irrespective of origins, to select the specific process improvement methodologies or techniques that best address the problems at hand and lead to the desired business results. That could even mean applying CMMI to manufacturing, or lean engineering to software development. Operations and service functions also follow processes that should be examined with an eye toward continuous improvement.

2.2.2 Nurturing a Continuous Improvement Culture

A culture of continuous improvement and innovation is a culture that embraces change. People at all levels in the organization routinely and frequently look for ways to improve. Because its environment is constantly changing, an organization that never changes is in danger of failing to understand the dynamic needs and desires of its customers and stakeholders. At the same time, change for the sake of change is both unsettling and counterproductive. Instead, the goal is to implement change that improves the ability of the organization to meet its business objectives. With a culture of continuous improvement, all employees (from upper management on down) know that they have a stake in the game. Every employee looks for opportunities to improve and welcome improvement suggestions from others. Everyone knows how he or she aligns with the goals of continuous improvement.[2]

Sometimes your customers—especially those who want you to succeed and improve—will establish requirements for your operations, such as having an ISO certification, demonstrating a CMMI maturity level, or developing a plan on how you intend to use lean engineering. For example, an ISO certification might be required to do business in some European countries, a CMMI appraisal at specified maturity or capability levels might be called out in an RFP to bid on a contract, or a subcontractor on a particular job might be required by an acquirer to execute a lean engineering plan. However, the benefits of focusing on process improvement extend far beyond your need to respond to such external encouragement.

From time to time, take the opportunity to think more clearly about what it really means to "embrace change." A culture of continuous improvement helps you to develop and maintain processes that will achieve the following goals:

- Improve program success and avoid crisis management
- Enable action on the root causes of persistent problems, making adjustments so that the same problems do not reappear again and again
- Institutionalize learning throughout the organization

---

2. It is extremely important that continuous improvement advocates don't become what Barry Boehm calls "change-averse change agents"!

To make this cultural shift become reality, continuous improvement initiatives must outline the various changes needed at all levels in the organization: senior management, program management, functional management, program personnel, and the champions for process improvement. In a smaller organization, many of these roles may be combined—and might even be yours.

2.2.3 Providing Strong Leadership

Cultural change in an organization requires top leadership at all levels to be engaged, accountable, and committed. Leaders should be ready to explain and defend from a business perspective the investment that they are making in continuous improvement. Their support must be strong, consistent, and visible to build a consensus among practitioners that the endeavor is not merely the management approach du jour. (Whatever happened to total quality management, anyway?)

Executive buy-in and support are critical to obtain resources for process improvement activities and to ensure rewards for the innovation and additional hard work required for change. When initiatives cut across organizations, executives must bridge the organizational gaps and soothe the bruised egos that inevitably appear in the course of multidisciplinary endeavors. Leadership must achieve consensus among both middle management and the practitioners; otherwise, process improvement will become a paper exercise that produces hollow artifacts and lackluster performance.

For these reasons, it is essential to get commitment from executives early and often. Help them construct the "elevator speech" they need to counter resistance from middle management.[3] Executives must "walk the talk" and understand that if they take actions that belie process improvement tenets, this seemingly subtle message will be heard just as loudly as public denigration of the program. Help them develop an ongoing communication strategy, achievable goals, and good metrics for their own performance plans that can trickle down to their direct reports. Above all, make sure that upper management is notified of early successes. These stories can be trotted out to defend

---

3. By an "elevator speech," we mean a brief summary of the goals, costs, and benefits of your project. This sales pitch should be short enough to be delivered effectively in the space of an elevator ride.

the program when the first wave of cash-flow problems, schedule adjustments, or other similar crisis occurs.

Leadership continuously focuses everyone on the big-picture goals:

- Processes must be best-in-class if business performance and growth demands are to be met.
- The process environment must rely on measurable data to deliver on commitments to customers.

The benefits of a skilled workforce and a strong process focus are realized best when managers lead the charge. Concentrate on keeping your executives aware, involved, and excited. If you do, you will be well on your way to a successful continuous improvement program.

2.2.4 Linking Improvement to Business Strategies and Results

Improvement efforts require organizational support and the allocation of resources. Those efforts should support stated business objectives and goals. Those who advocate specific process improvement projects have the obligation to make explicit the link between those projects and the organization's stated business strategies. If a specific process improvement activity can improve the chances of winning critical business in the future, it is more likely to be embraced.

Some improvements target cost savings; others tackle cost avoidance. Process improvement will have more success, however, if a majority of those improvements directly target cost savings. Simply put, the resources expended on a specific process improvement effort should be offset by the future savings that will result from instituting the change. A convincing business case for this should be made before starting any larger-scale process improvement effort.[4] In particular, each process improvement effort that exceeds a certain size threshold should have a project charter that provides a business case.

A successful process improvement proposal will detail which data is to be collected, how that data is to be used, and what the measure of success will be; it will make a clear business case for the change. Having

---

4. Many smaller improvements (e.g., removing an unneeded step from a process) should not be burdened with the task of creating a business case for such change. Having a lot of managerial requirements for simple process improvements will discourage people from making those improvements.

good data available to support business decisions and to run programs well is a central goal of any continuous improvement initiative. Senior management may listen politely when well-meaning individuals state their fervent beliefs about why some change should be made, but it is the appropriate collection, analysis, and use of data that is likely to win approval and maintain management commitment to the activity.

2.2.5 Focusing on the Customer

In recent years, virtually all of the major process improvement initiatives have emphasized the importance of focusing on customer value and on managing customer expectations. Six Sigma, lean engineering, and CMMI, for example, share this feature.

For instance, listening to the voice of the customer (VOC) is an essential component of the Six Sigma methodology. Typically, the defects that Six Sigma projects seek to correct manifest themselves in a failure to meet a measurable customer requirement. An important aspect of any Six Sigma improvement is its impact on customer satisfaction and how it adds value to the customer by better meeting the customer requirements.

Similarly, one of the 12 overarching principles in the Lean Enterprise Model (LEM) is having a continuous focus on the customers. Within the LEM, emphasis is placed on the following concerns:

- Having stable and cooperative relationships with customers and suppliers
- Including customers on integrated product teams
- Being proactive to understand and respond to the needs of internal and external customers
- Providing insight for customers into the metrics used by suppliers
- Sharing information with customers
- Having customers involved in requirements generation, product design, and problem solving
- Having strategies to deal with customer changes

An essential theme within the CMMI models is the identification and involvement of all key project stakeholders, where "stakeholder" is understood to mean a group or individual that is affected by or in some way accountable for the outcome of an undertaking. Stakeholders may include project members, suppliers, customers, and end users. In CMMI,

Integrated Product and Process Development (IPPD) is defined as a systematic approach that achieves a timely collaboration of relevant stakeholders throughout the life of the product in an attempt to better satisfy customer needs, expectations, and requirements, including quality objectives.

In CMMI, the customer appears in many contexts. Customer needs are viewed as essential to defining quantitative process objectives. The requirements development process in CMMI is characterized as transforming customer needs into product requirements, whereas final validation of the product focuses on whether customer needs have been met. Process improvement activities are to be undertaken in part because of their effects on customer satisfaction. A part of project planning entails addressing all the commitments that have been undertaken with the customer. Information from progress reviews should be communicated to customers, as well as the status of program risks. As in the LEM, in CMMI customers should be considered for inclusion in integrated product teams. During all stages of product development, life-cycle cost issues should be brought to the attention of the customers. In all of these areas of the CMMI model, as well as in others, what customers want and need is paramount.

Having seen how Six Sigma, lean engineering, and CMMI all value the role of the customer, we must also issue a call for common sense: Anything—even a customer focus—can be overdone. For example, care must be taken when customer views are undeveloped, inconsistent, or just plain wrong. It is not a good idea to unthinkingly accept everything that the customer says is needed, and the effects of a customer's change of mind on cost, schedule, and quality must be carefully examined. Even with these provisos, however, continuous improvement should always be undertaken (as the Six Sigma, lean engineering, and CMMI approaches indicate) with a close eye maintained on customers. Indeed, careful consideration is needed from the start regarding not just the benefits that improvement efforts might provide to a customer, but also the role a customer might play in those continuous improvement efforts.

2.2.6 Making Quality as Important as Cost and Schedule

For many years and in many business contexts, discussions about quality and the importance of an organizational focus on quality have generated strong interest. To highlight one example, for many years the U.S. automobile industry has strived to improve both the quality of its products and consumers' recognition of that improved product quality. Clearly something still is missing, as the U.S. domestic market share in this industry continues its slide. We may surmise that this slide will be reversed only after both quality products and consumers' recognition of quality are firmly entrenched.

Needless to say, quality does not stand alone. We are all familiar with the sign in the print shop: "Good, Fast, Cheap: Pick Any Two." In other words, a good product with fast service will not come cheaply; a fast and cheap product will not have the highest quality; and a good product at a reduced cost may be obtained, if one is willing to be patient. Of course, it is easy for a shop owner to pronounce with authority (and advertise) that he provides his customers with all three: good, fast, and cheap. Nevertheless, such a pronouncement does not make it easier to do in the real world.

In many industries, a similar list of three items might be this: cost, schedule, and quality. In this case, it is clear that we do strive for all three: meet the financial targets, deliver the product on time, and have the end result meet the customer's expectations for a quality product. However, on a daily basis we tend not to give the quality dimension equal emphasis. While cost and schedule issues are objects of incessant attention, aspects of product quality (including product performance, reliability, supportability, and field availability) are often the subject of less intense monitoring. In the end, a project may compromise on quality to achieve cost and schedule objectives.

In a culture characterized by continuous improvement, quality is the responsibility of everyone. Quality shortcomings are prime candidates for the scrutiny of a process improvement project. Indeed, any candidate process-improvement project should be evaluated in part based on how it affects both the quality of products and customers' recognition of that quality. It is especially important to make sure that the processes contributing to better quality are not (easily or routinely) compromised as a result of cost and schedule pressures.

2.2.7 Establishing Criteria for Larger Improvement Events

So far, we have discussed various aspects of an improvement project. Clearly, not all of the activities that relate to improvement occur in the context of a formal and organized project. If you are doing your job and collecting data to monitor your progress, and that data tells you that an adjustment is needed, you do not need a large and expensive team of experts to help you fix the problem. At the other end of the spectrum, if a problem could have a major impact on the business—one that will require study and investigation to understand both the extent of the problem and its root causes—then running a project-like activity is needed. Multi-month, multi-person activities need formal criteria to prioritize and authorize the outlay of resources.

Here is the kind of information typically required in a proposal for a large-scale process improvement event:

- Current problem
- Approach to improvement, including tools to be used
- Resources needed
- Areas to be improved
- Anticipated benefits
- Risk analysis
- Schedule, with termination criteria
- Effect on customers and other key stakeholders
- Metrics to be used
- Options for employee recognition
- Link to business strategy

Templates that outline all of the required information are useful in planning such a project. In considering the continuum of small and large process-improvement projects, it is the larger ones that tend to need the full criteria set. For smaller improvements or in smaller organizations, just making sure that the effort and resources are consistent with the expected payoff may be sufficient.

2.3 Five Keys for Continuous Improvement

In the past, process improvement initiatives have existed in stovepipes associated with specific techniques. That is, there were lean engineering advocates, ISO quality experts, CMMI enthusiasts, and so on. Our integrated viewpoint, however, has moved us to a more methodology-independent level. We can look across all of the tools and techniques in all of these initiatives, and select the unique set of approaches that best meets our needs.

The five keys that we discuss in this section are not keys to five separate doors; rather, it is their use in appropriate combinations that will open various doors on the path to continuous change and improvement. When improvements are undertaken using a single approach, the "big picture" for process improvement is obscured. By integrating the various tools and methodologies, we are able to address a wider array of problems than if we stayed within the process improvement box with which we happen to have the most familiarity.

2.3.1 Process Excellence

From a strategic point of view, the first "key" of process excellence involves nurturing a culture of continuous improvement, while identifying and using appropriate tools and methodologies to improve your processes. The other four "keys" (discussed in Sections 2.3.2 to 2.3.5) are examples of such tools and methods (Figure 2-1).

An infrastructure for process excellence allows process knowledge to be used to improve the business. A process library holds the organization's policies, process requirements, procedures, guidance, and related process information (e.g., templates, checklists). Most organizations will develop multiple processes to meet the needs of all the kinds of projects that they do—large or small, normal or time critical, and so

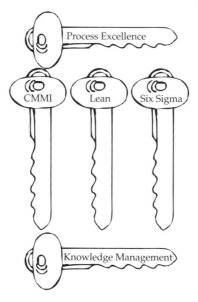

Figure 2-1: *Five keys for continuous improvement*

forth. Guidance in applying the appropriate process in a given situation is extremely important.

Process excellence relies on the identification of both successful and unsuccessful practices, and on the use of lessons learned; these two go hand-in-hand. Suppose that some process change has been identified that, if it were more widely practiced, would bring a significant competitive advantage (via cost savings, reduced cycle time, or some other criterion). In one scenario, a successful practice (or lesson learned) is stored somewhere so that potential benefactors who want to improve their own operations can search for improvement ideas. In another scenario, a group—a committee, council, or integrated process team (IPT)—that oversees a successful practice actively identifies potential benefactors throughout the organization and "pushes" the information out to them in an effort to maximize the potential benefits. Of course, in the case of unsuccessful practices, warnings—rather than kudos—are recorded or communicated.

The best way to derive value from lessons learned and successful practices is not just to list them, but to incorporate them into the standard processes and procedures by which business is routinely conducted. This should be a central activity in any culture of continuous improvement. Those who champion improvements to standard processes should be recognized for their efforts.

To understand the effects of process improvement, process performance must be measured and monitored. While the extent to which defined processes are followed is important, the extent to which they contribute to meeting business objectives and delivering value to your customers is even more telling. When changes are made, they must be implemented and deployed correctly to ensure that they deliver their full value to the organization. Business priorities and gaps drive process improvement activities. The process monitoring infrastructure is in place to ensure that all the necessary support activities needed to realize the expected benefits occur. For instance, if you improve one process but don't take into consideration adverse effects on enabling or dependent processes, as well as the effects of the change on users, you may actually see a reduction in business performance.[5]

---

5. A classic example would be improvements to a company's ordering system that meet the stated goals, but that fail to account for how those changes affect subsequent processes. While the ordering system "improves," the product delivery system may fail to respond to the orders in a timely manner.

Usually primary process performance indicators (such as product quality, schedule, cycle time, and productivity, and the impact that these may have on customer satisfaction and cost) are used to measure the effectiveness of a process improvement program. Improvements related to these indicators typically support the achievement of company business goals, which may include increased profitability or larger market share.

By identifying which performance indicators are to be targeted for improvement, and then selecting process improvement projects that focus on those indicators, you are in a position to begin the calculation of business value and return on investment (ROI) from the project. To quantify the benefit associated with an indicator, you need to specify an appropriate metric, such as defects per unit, hours per unit, days for the project, costs saved or costs avoided, or a customer satisfaction score. You can convert these metrics into dollar amounts, based on the value of hours saved, the amount of additional business garnered, or the amount of additional profit generated, for example. Similarly, you need to quantify the cost of the improvement activity, including purchases, development work, training, maintenance, and fees. Finally, by dividing the financial benefits by the financial costs, and then subtracting 1, you can compute the ROI. For example, if an effort cost $50,000 and had a benefit of $50,000, there would be a 0 percent ROI. By contrast, if an effort that cost $50,000 had a benefit of $100,000, the project would have a 100 percent ROI.[6]

One industry standard whose use may promote process excellence is ISO 9000. Actually, this certification comprises a family of standards that represents good management practices to ensure an organization can consistently deliver products or services that meet its customers' quality requirements. Within the ISO 9000 family of standards, ISO 9001:2000 is the one that contains process requirements; it covers these five areas:

- Quality management systems
- Management responsibility
- Resource management
- Product realization
- Measurement, analysis, and improvement

---

6. ROI may be expressed also as a ratio. The result of the first example stated in this manner would be 1:1 ROI, and the second would be 2:1 ROI.

There is substantial overlap between the requirements in these five areas and the process requirements in CMMI. While some differences in coverage exist, in general we predict that an organization that meets CMMI requirements will likely meet most ISO 9001:2000 requirements, and (to a lesser extent) vice versa.

2.3.2 CMMI

Capability Maturity Model Integration (CMMI), which is the principle topic of this book, comprises a framework for coordinating process improvement efforts across an enterprise and measuring and monitoring the status of those efforts. Given that we will describe CMMI in detail in Part II of this book, here we will offer only a brief exposition of this model.

The CMMI provides a basis for benchmarking the "capability" of individual processes and the "maturity" of organizational efforts relating to process. One distinctive feature of CMMI is its use of "levels" to measure both of these things: the capability of an organization in individual process areas (from capability level 0 to capability level 5, with capability level 5 being best), and an overall organizational process maturity rating (from maturity level 1 to maturity level 5, with maturity level 5 being best).

Periodic CMMI appraisals can provide a broad-brush scorecard indicating where process strengths and weaknesses exist, and which areas deserve attention in future process improvement planning. The teams that are formed to conduct a CMMI appraisal are usually led by someone from outside the organization being appraised. This must be the case when level values are assigned; the independence of the lead appraiser guards against any biased ratings. In contrast, the members of the team who come from within the organization being appraised play important roles in helping the team understand the processes within the user's context and interpret the organization's vocabulary. It is these team members who have sufficient knowledge of the organization to probe it for process weaknesses and strengths.

2.3.3 Lean Engineering

The lean engineering approach to process improvement is a result of the Lean Advancement Initiative (LAI), a U.S. consortium of government, industry, labor, and academic institutions. In the early 1990s, the U.S. Air Force began to ask whether the advances that had been made in lean-engineering automobile production in Japan could be applied to the U.S. aerospace industry. As a result, LAI was started at the Massachusetts Institute of Technology (MIT) in 1993 to help reduce the cost of producing aircraft and other aerospace products. The Lean Enterprise Model focuses on the reduction of waste to improve the flow of information and work products, and the efficient creation of value for the enterprise.

Similar to other process improvement methods, a basic premise of lean engineering is that there is always a better way to provide products and services by continuously improving operations. Managers and employees learn to question the need for every work-sequence motion, for every item of in-process stock, and for every second that people, material, or machines are idle.

Some Basic Lean Engineering Concepts

One foundation for creating a lean enterprise involves using a "six S" approach to create a safe workplace suited for visual order and control:

- *Sort.* Keep only the necessary tools, parts, and instructions.
- *Straighten.* Arrange items neatly and orderly.
- *Shine.* Visually sweep area and conduct cleanup to facilitate the identification of abnormalities.
- *Standardize.* Consistently apply the sort, straighten, and shine methods.
- *Sustain.* Properly maintain the correct procedures.
- *Safety.* Identify and eliminate dangerous and hazardous conditions.

Within an enterprise, lean engineering can be applied to all activities in which there could be inefficiency in how things are done. The LEM includes 12 overarching practices:

- Identify and optimize enterprise flow
- Implement integrated product and process development
- Maintain the challenge of existing processes
- Ensure seamless information flow

(continued)

> ### *Some Basic Lean Engineering Concepts (continued)*
>
> - Ensure process capability and maturation
> - Maximize stability in a changing environment
> - Optimize capability and utilization of people
> - Develop relationships based on mutual trust, commitment, and accountability
> - Nurture a learning environment
> - Make decisions at the lowest possible level
> - Promote lean leadership at all levels
> - Continuously focus on the customers

A key activity in a lean engineering approach is to focus on the process steps by which "value" is added to work products. A step that moves one toward the functionality of a product or service that is valued by a customer is a "value-added" step, whereas a step that does not is "non-value-added." A mapping of the "value stream" is created to depict all of the process steps used in creating the product, some of which may add value and some of which may not. For each step, the extent to which "value" is added to the product is determined. The central objective is to use this analysis to reduce the time during which no value is added, such as a part sitting unused for days in a queue during a manufacturing process.[7]

A complete value-stream map of a process is called a "current-state map." To reduce the number of non-value-added steps in a process is to "eliminate waste." It is through the elimination of waste that one tries to move from the current-state map to a "future-state vision." [8]

Here are some key principles for any lean engineering journey:

- Understand "value" from the view of a customer.
- Map the value stream to make it visible to all stakeholders.

---

7. Three indications that an activity adds value are these: (1) The customer wants it and is willing to pay for it; (2) it changes the product or service; and (3) it is done right the first time, with no rework.

8. Most discussions of lean engineering identify multiple categories or types of waste. Typical categories include overproduction, inventory, waiting, transportation, motion, overprocessing, defects, reprioritization, and people skill utilization. Where you find one type of waste, expect to find others; they tend to snowball!

- Use the map to identify waste and increase value flow.
- Make changes to have value "pulled" from upstream in the process rather than "pushed" to the next step.
- Pursue perfection as a journey and not a destination.

For example, in a large organization it may take on the average six weeks to get an international travel request approved. In this case the traveler is the customer. A mapping of the current state for the travel approval process may show that 12 signatures are needed for international trips, and that paper is passed sequentially to 12 different individuals. Much of the time during the six weeks is taken up with the non-value-added activities of mailing the request from one location to another and having the request sit in an in-box somewhere awaiting a signature.

A future-state vision for this process may be to get a decision on the travel request within four working days, on average. Perhaps the needed signatures could be reduced from 12 to 4 without jeopardizing any needed oversight or checks or exposing the company to any unnecessary risk. Perhaps some of the signature approvals could be received concurrently instead of serially. Perhaps an electronic distribution would be speedier than relying on the company mail system. By mapping the value stream with experts and process owners and identifying the non-value-added steps, one can chart a course for improving this process.[9]

For an operation to be and stay lean, managers should frequent the venues in which value is created for the organization. They should ask questions about problems and their causes, help employees understand that they have management support for their efforts to solve the problem, and make sure everyone understands which data would be used to show that the problem has been addressed.[10]

2.3.4 Six Sigma

Six Sigma is an improvement methodology developed and used by Motorola, Texas Instruments, General Electric, Allied Signal, Lockheed Martin, Honeywell, and many other companies. The popularity of the Six Sigma model is due in part to the publicity regarding former

---

9. It is interesting to see how different improvement initiatives can bring different perspectives to the table. In lean engineering, frequently an inspection is viewed as a non-value-added activity, one that should be eliminated. In CMMI, software inspections are viewed as a successful practice, one that should be emulated. Hmmm, eliminate or emulate inspections?
10. For more information about lean engineering, go to http://lean.mit.edu.

General Electric CEO Jack Welch and his commitment to achieving Six Sigma capability. The Six Sigma methodology and tools are applicable to any process, including manufacturing, services, and engineering.

Six Sigma has four major objectives: (1) maintain control of process, (2) improve constantly, (3) exceed customer expectations, and (4) add tangibly to the bottom line. This methodology brings with it several tools, such as failure modes and effect analysis (FMEA), regression analysis, process simulation, and control charts. Within the Six Sigma framework there is an explicit use of statistical tools to understand and address process variation.

One central concept is analyzing a process, measuring the number of defects that may occur, and then systematically working to determine how to improve the process so as to eliminate as much as possible the causes of defects. Defects are defined as anything outside of customer specifications. To achieve the Six Sigma goals, a process must not produce more than 3.4 defects per 1 million opportunities, where an opportunity is defined as an action with a chance for a defect.

There are several Six Sigma improvement methodologies, the most widely used of which is called DMAIC (dŭ·mā·ĭk), which stands for five process steps: define, measure, analyze, improve, and control. Figure 2-2 illustrates the key Six Sigma concepts.

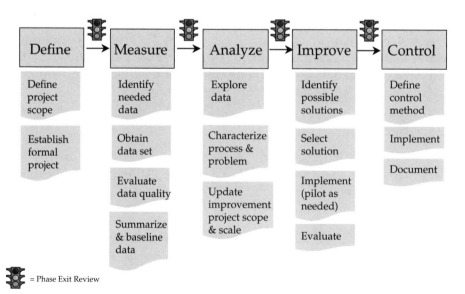

Figure 2-2: *The Six Sigma DMAIC method*

Define. The Six Sigma team defines the project's purpose and scope, creating a project charter as a contract between the organization's leadership and the team. The charter contains (for example) the problem statement, the business case for the project, the scope, the roles of the various team members, the milestones, and the required resources. The team obtains information on the customer (the voice of the customer [VOC]) and uses this data to develop a list of CTQs (critical to quality), CTCs (critical to cost), and CTDs (critical to delivery). More generally, we refer to all three of these components as CTX analysis. CTXs are requirements necessary for a product or service to fulfill the needs of a customer. Basic facts about the processes to be improved are captured using SIPOC (an acronym for "suppliers, inputs, processes, outputs, and customers"). In other words, SIPOC defines which inputs are needed for the process and who supplies those inputs, and which outputs are produced by the process and who makes use of those outputs.

The team may also identify "key characteristics," which are features of a product or process whose variation may play a key role in product fit, performance, service life, manufacturability, or some other central requirement. If a key characteristic is not being met, you may need to consider a redesign, or better process control, or better inspection and testing.

Measure. The team measures the performance of the current process relative to the CTXs. The goal is to collect data relating to a process, to identify defects that are produced by the process, and to determine the possible causes of those defects. A variety of methods are available to collect, organize, and display the data. It is at this stage that the existing process is characterized and mapped, a baseline is defined, and the process capability is determined.

Analyze. The team identifies and verifies the underlying root causes of the defects produced by the existing process and quantifies their effects. Tools such as fishbone charts are useful in identifying the various causes and interdependencies at work in producing defects. Correlation and regression analysis, hypothesis testing, and statistical process control (SPC) are other methods of analyzing process data. The goal in this step is to identify sources of variation.

Improve. The team screens the potential causes of variation, reviews variable relationships, and optimizes the process. Improvement actions are identified and plans are established based on a cost–benefit analysis. Changes may be implemented in pilot tests to determine their effectiveness.

Control. The team validates the measurement system, determines the new process capability, and ensures that process controls are in place for monitoring and controlling the new process. The gains expected from the implemented changes are measured and maintained. Once the value of the new process has been documented, the results are made available to the process owner. And, of course, the team celebrates its success.

One way to think about Six Sigma, and its relationship with lean engineering and CMMI, is to focus on three key, interconnected process features: maturity, efficiency, and control. In general terms, maturity models such as CMMI focus on the maturity and capability of processes, lean engineering focuses on process efficiency and the removal of waste, and Six Sigma addresses process control and the reduction of process variability. It should be obvious that your toolkit for continuous improvement could benefit from including tools that help with all three aspects: maturity, efficiency, and control.

2.3.5 Knowledge Management

The somewhat formal title of "knowledge management" (KM) means simply managing data and information for the organization to promote its value as a shared resource. The goal of KM is to make relevant organizational knowledge available to those who need it, when they need it. To accomplish this task, an organization needs to have processes and tools in place to facilitate the flow of information. The larger the organization, the more "knowledge" there is, and the more daunting the management challenge. The effective use of organizational knowledge can have many beneficial results—improved performance and competitiveness, better sharing of successful practices, and better team collaboration, to name a few.

There are many ways in which a culture of continuous learning and improvement depends on the effective management of organizational knowledge. If an important lesson learned is not known by those for whom it would be useful, prior mistakes could be repeated. If information about corporate strategic goals is not widely disseminated, business decisions could be out of alignment and might run counter to each other. If insight into customer preferences is lacking, one of the prime targets for process improvement could be misunderstood. We can facilitate continuous improvement activities by working toward the KM goal of having organizational knowledge available to people when they need it.

In many organizations, one important aspect of KM is knowledge retention. As a workforce ages and members with expert knowledge approach retirement, a challenge that emerges is the need to assure that critical knowledge is not lost to the organization. One response to this issue is simple: hire retirees back as independent contractors. While this plan can have many benefits, it is helpful to supplement it with a more comprehensive approach to the issue, including mentoring of new talent by the experts, requiring succession planning, and requiring knowledge transfer planning and execution.

2.3.6 Using the Five Keys to Continuous Improvement

Starting in Chapter 3, we will explore in detail one of the five keys to continuous improvement: CMMI. Our brief discussion here is intended to encourage current and potential CMMI users to adopt an expansive view toward continuous process improvement. You need to strive for process excellence and a culture amenable to continuous improvement by developing indicators that help you achieve your business objectives. A variety of improvement strategies are available to you in the tools and techniques offered through ISO, CMMI, lean engineering, and Six Sigma, as well as other methods. You need to look at the big picture and not just CMMI. Good management of your knowledge resources is a critical foundation for any improvement strategy.

2.4 Management of Continuous Improvement Activities

Typically in larger organizations, multiple groups are responsible for coordinating continuous improvement. Their objective is to define and implement a coordinated and integrated approach to continuous process improvement in certain areas.[11] Such groups may have the following responsibilities:

* Creating and sustaining a framework for continuous improvement that is focused on customers and quality, data driven, linked to business strategy, and tied to business results
* Establishing and promoting a culture of continuous learning and improvement across the organization

---

11. Of course in a smaller organization there may be only one group or even just one person assuming the responsibilities outlined here.

- Identifying, evaluating, promoting, and supporting the deployment of appropriate continuous improvement methodologies, practices, and tools, such as those currently used in (but not limited to) lean engineering, Six Sigma, ISO, and CMMI initiatives
- Identifying and sharing successful practices across the organization
- Establishing common definitions, methodologies, and standards for process management
- Developing qualified practitioners to participate in process improvement initiatives
- Developing common criteria and metrics to evaluate the viability and business benefits of process improvement initiatives
- Developing and maintaining a set of leading indicators
- Providing insight and recommendations to the senior staff of the organization to advance continuous improvement
- Helping the practitioners apply the processes in an efficient, effective, and locally controlled way

It is critical to establish the roles and responsibilities for those individuals who will lead, train, and perform the process improvement activities. This infrastructure becomes even more crucial when the organization is approaching continuous improvement in an integrated fashion. Generally, a cadre of process champions will provide the core energy, experience, and initial sweat and blood to get process improvement off the ground. These people, however, may not represent all of the stakeholders or power centers that will have important roles in the fully integrated environment.

Be aware of the political ramifications of integrating process improvement activities when forming your process groups. Make sure that all of the organizations involved have a place at the table; their participation will help counter the idea that the initiative is "something being done to them" against their wishes. Hold open meetings and advertise the outcomes. Also, keep a sense of equity throughout the effort—everyone should share in the rewards as well as the responsibility and the work.

The steering group should not be limited to practitioners and process improvement specialists. Instead, it will prove much more effective if middle management is included and if executive management is represented or chairs the group. In this way, the process-oriented groups can adequately deal with resource and other management issues, and the process champions can lead by example. The steering group should provide a feedback mechanism for the process practitioners.

Similarly, a process group that comprises mostly managers probably will not get the nitty-gritty work done. To achieve its goals, it will need subgroups, committees, or work teams to coordinate necessary training, build better processes, maintain process assets, and perform all the other activities involved in process improvement. From the outset, make sure that sufficient resources and guidance are available to allow these groups to function reasonably autonomously. Otherwise, you'll end up with your steering group micromanaging process improvement, and chaos waiting at the doorstep.

For both the steering group and the work teams, it is important to recognize that team development is a crucial step. It takes time for team members to get up to speed; to define and understand their roles, responsibilities, expectations, and outcomes; and to recognize and address each member's wants and needs. Strong leadership can help steer the course through both smooth and rough waters.

Skill development is probably one of the more expensive—and more important—aspects of the infrastructure. With integrated process improvement, the required skills and training go beyond simple process definition, facilitation, and model comprehension courses; they extend into the various disciplines involved as well. Software, hardware, and systems engineers may need to be cross-trained. They certainly need to understand the fundamentals of one another's disciplines to define effective processes that involve all three areas. Although most organizations have internal resources that can provide much of this training, others may need to look into local university courses or professional training resources. Whatever way you acquire those resources, the quality, timeliness, and relevance of the training and other skill development activities can have enormous implications for the success of your program.

2.5 Everyone Understands and Participates

One cornerstone of any continuous improvement effort is having each manager and employee understand the processes that apply to the tasks at hand, and having them perform those tasks in a manner consistent with the defined processes. Questions about the processes that you should be following may be addressed simply by reading the process documentation or by availing yourself of training courses or expert mentoring. Everyone should have an understanding of the processes they are expected to follow to do their job, including both those processes specific to their current assignment and the standard processes that everyone is to follow.

If someone in the organization finds that the current defined process is faulty, inefficient, or otherwise obstructing job performance, that person should initiate a change request or otherwise raise the issue to get the process updated. Ineffective processes on the books help no one. Often there is a necessary give-and-take between those who want elaborate processes in place to guard against potential problems and those who on a day-in, day-out basis work to get product out the door and who may find certain process requirements burdensome.[12] It is a continuous activity for all of us to constantly refine our organization's defined processes so that they are not burdensome and are viewed as a positive force in getting the job done right.

An organization may not need a large cadre of full-time process improvement experts. While a few such people may provide needed benefit, the contrast between those who "work projects" and those who "work process" needs to evolve. In short, we need people with a sufficient amount of real-world project experiences to be leaders in the effort to improve the processes; otherwise, we put the success of the process improvement effort at risk. Some organizations are moving toward a rotation system where employees "do tours" in multiple areas to increase the competency of both those who work projects and those who work process. Of course, fundamentally, everyone in the organization should be an improver!

At the same time, to run Six Sigma projects, an organization needs Green Belts, Black Belts, and Master Black Belts. A Master Black Belt may have the training and experience to justify a nearly full-time focus on process improvement; for most people who are trained to the Green Belt or Black Belt level, however, this may be an occasional or part-time effort. Similarly, to contribute to a value-stream mapping, an organization may need knowledgeable people with an appropriate degree of understanding and experience in lean engineering. To participate on a CMMI or ISO appraisal, we need an appropriate number of lead appraisers and trainers who can help prepare and guide the activity,

---

12. A good example is trade studies and the requirement to document important decisions and their rationale. Those working an effort may not want to expend the resources needed to document a decision, whereas those who inherit a program that is in trouble may wish they had a better understanding of decisions made earlier in the program's history.

and then educate those who will participate in the appraisal regarding what is expected of them. Very few of these assignments require a full-time commitment. For those who in varying degrees work on activities related to continuous improvement, a community of practice (CoP) may be established to help them to share their knowledge and experiences.

As you strive to embed continuous improvement into your organizational culture, you will need to provide specific guidance to all employees—from new hires all the way to the most experienced staff. This educational effort should include the steps to be taken if an employee wishes to participate on a more formalized continuous improvement activity, the organization's current needs in terms of process improvement skills, training options, manager approvals needed, and so on.

2.6 Pearls of Wisdom

In this chapter, we have recommended an expansive, inclusive, and integrated approach to continuous improvement. Nevertheless, you should not assume that by becoming a CMMI expert you will have all you need to improve processes and your business.

Perhaps you are part of an organization that has performed admirably in recent years while many of your competitors have faltered. Perhaps your products are well accepted; perhaps you already have established and well-documented processes; perhaps you already enjoy a good market share and high levels of customer satisfaction. So you have been—and are—doing something right; in fact, you may be doing a lot that is right. Given this enviable position, why do you want to embark on a new effort to "continuously improve"? Why do you want to "tinker" with a profit-generating machine that is working quite well? What is the risk of change? What is wrong with the status quo?

The answers to these questions are not hard to understand: However successful you have been, you should strive to do better. To remain competitive, you may *need* to do better. One of the cornerstones of the continuous improvement is the link with business strategies, and a focus on business results. To lay a strong foundation for "doing better," you should take the following steps:

- Study problems that affect both your customers and your profitability

- Make improvements that put your organization in a better position to obtain future business
- See that the savings realized from improvement projects pay back the outlay to run those projects and, in addition, provide a significant supplemental return
- Champion changes that support your doing a better job of meeting your programs' quality, cost, and schedule objectives

We conclude this chapter with some brief practical advice, or "pearls of wisdom." These ideas are intended to help you keep in mind some general issues as you start to learn more about CMMI.

- Support an integrated structure for continuous improvement groups.
- Build accountability into every step, at every level.
- Manage "experts and zealots" carefully—they can sometimes raise more barriers than they overcome.
- Integrate continuous improvement reviews into project management reviews and individual performance evaluations.
- Capture the hearts of middle managers.
- Create continuous improvement as a core competency within the organization; hire for it, recognize it, reward it.
- Understand that the devil is in the details—make sure that the implementation is as strong and coherent as the vision.
- Train to organizational processes so that future changes to improvement models, standards, and other facets of the improvement process will have smaller effects on the organization.
- Conduct regular process appraisals that emphasize proactive improvement, replacing the audit philosophy and decreasing the fear factor.
- Engage real process users who can force the process definitions to be user-friendly and to address real-world, multidisciplinary concerns.
- Encourage process users to "own" their processes and take pride in using and improving them.
- Employ a well-designed cost accounting system to facilitate the collection of useful process metrics data, particularly for cross-functional activities.

- Make a focused, continuing effort to identify common improvement opportunities.

- Use a "workshop" approach to process engineering, which can result in a tenfold increase in productivity for typical meetings.

- Use pilot projects early in any effort to create an integrated process, thereby allowing for testing and fine-tuning. A good cross-section of projects gives early feedback on where improvements are needed.

- Don't try to integrate organizations that differ widely in their process capabilities or maturity levels. Work first on process basics with groups that are just starting out on the journey.

- Fight the "Not invented here" syndrome. "Steal with pride" is a better motto.

- Focus on the development of a straightforward and consistent method for tailoring standard processes, especially for organizations that include highly diverse project domains. Even better, organize your process assets so that "standard" processes are very close to every type of project you might encounter (such as safety-critical processes, schedule-critical processes, processes using agile or other nontraditional development methods, and legacy product maintenance).

- Remember that almost any change in an integrated environment will affect other groups. John Donne was right: "No man is an island."

- Recognize that an integrated, cross-disciplinary improvement effort may identify many issues and rivalries, and you will need to find creative ways to address them.

- Strive for improvements that prevent the sub-optimization of processes in a cross-disciplinary environment.

- Strive for cross-disciplinary continuous improvements that yield more accurate project planning and reduced cycle time.

- Work to increase the buy-in from all affected organizations as you develop an integrated approach to improvement.

- Implement integrated engineering assets as part of your efforts in continuous improvement.

Now, don't you feel wiser already? On to CMMI!

Chesapeake Bay Area
LandSat 5 Thematic Mapper (1998)
NASA—Goddard Space Flight Center
Scientific Visualization Studio

Part II

The CMMI Models

The Chesapeake Bay is a highly productive economic engine. It is also a fragile ecosystem. Its best use and long-term prospects depend on making decisions that are based on an understanding of the complex relationships that exist between nature and humans.

Similarly, CMMI products are complex structures containing multiple layers of information. To achieve the highest benefit, CMMI users need to be aware of this complexity and the subtle relationships between and across the information layers. In Part II of this book, we discuss the CMMI architecture and components, to help the reader more clearly understand how CMMI is structured and how its parts relate to one another and to integrated continuous improvement as a whole.

Part II Contents

Chapter 3. The CMMI Concept

In which the reader is introduced to CMMI—its contents, objectives, limitations, accomplishments, and history.

Chapter 4. CMMI Content

In which we describe the various elements and materials found in the CMMI models. Their relative importance is discussed to some extent, and the locations of the materials are elucidated.

Chapter 5. CMMI Representations

In which we describe two model representations—staged and continuous—and explain how they are accomplished within CMMI. A discussion of how the continuous representation can approximate the staged representation is presented.

Chapter 6. CMMI Dimensions for Measuring Improvement

In which we explain the manner by which the CMMI models—in both representations—guide and measure the improvement of processes. Both the capability and maturity dimensions are addressed. The concept of generic practices is introduced and their role in CMMI explained.

Chapter 7. CMMI Process Areas

In which the CMMI process dimension is described in detail, so that the practitioner may understand the relationship between the goals, practices, and improvement dimensions.

Chapter 3

The CMMI Concept

It must be remembered that there is nothing more difficult to plan,
more uncertain of success, nor more dangerous to manage than the
creation of a new order of things. For the initiator has the enmity of all
who would profit by the preservation of the old institutions, and merely
lukewarm defenders in those who would gain by the new order.
Machiavelli, *The Prince* (1513)

In this age, which believes that there is a short cut to everything,
the greatest lesson to be learned is that the most difficult way is,
in the long run, the easiest.
Henry Miller, *The Books in My Life* (1957)

The implementation of continuous improvement in an organization is possible using two or more single-discipline models. There are many advantages, however, in having just one model that covers multiple disciplines. For this reason, the U.S. Department of Defense—specifically, the Under Secretary of Defense for Acquisition, Technology, and Logistics—teamed up with the National Defense Industrial Association (NDIA) to jointly sponsor the development of Capability Maturity Model Integration (CMMI). In 2000, under the stewardship of the Software Engineering Institute (SEI) at Carnegie Mellon University, this effort produced the first integrated CMMI models, together with associated appraisal and training materials. The year 2002 saw the release of CMMI version 1.1. Version 1.2 was released in 2006.

This chapter begins with an overview of the kinds of information and guidance found in CMMI models. For those not familiar with any of the source models, it provides a good introduction to CMMI's scope and usefulness. We follow this overview with a discussion of CMMI objectives and history. Next comes information on the source models that were used in creating CMMI. Finally, we describe the CMMI project organization.

3.1 An Overview of CMMI

The CMMI Product Suite contains an enormous amount of information and guidance to help an organization improve its processes. But how does this information help? To answer this question, we start by noting that the CMMI models contain essentially two kinds of materials:

* Materials to help you evaluate the content of your processes—information that is essential to your technical, support, and managerial activities
* Materials to help you improve process performance—information that is used to increase the capability of your organization's activities

We start with a brief look at each of these types of materials.

3.1.1 Process Content

CMMI provides guidance for your managerial processes. For example, you should establish and maintain a plan for managing your work, and make sure everyone involved is committed to performing and supporting the plan. When you plan, you should define exactly how you will develop and maintain cost, schedule, and product estimates. When you do the work that you have planned, you should compare the performance and progress against the plan, and initiate corrective actions if actual and planned results are out of synch. You should establish and maintain agreements with your suppliers and make sure that both parties satisfy them. CMMI also incorporates information on managing project risk and on creating and managing teams.

CMMI guidance on technical matters includes ways to develop, derive, and manage requirements, and to develop technical solutions that meet those requirements. The integration of product components depends on good interface information, and CMMI reminds us that integration activities need to be planned and verified. In following the CMMI model, you should make sure that the products and services you develop are consistent with their original requirements and satisfy the customer's needs through verification and validation practices.

Support processes for technical and managerial activities are also addressed as part of CMMI. You should always manage the versions and configurations of intermediate work products as well as end products and services. You should have methods for ensuring that the processes you have defined are followed and the products you are developing meet the quality specifications you have established. You need to decide which information is important and establish ways to measure and track it. In some cases, you need to plan ways to resolve issues formally. You may need to figure out the root cause of serious problems with your products or key processes.

3.1.2 Process Improvement

Once processes have been established, improving them becomes a key goal. The improvement information in CMMI models includes the creation of a viable, improvable process infrastructure. To build this infrastructure, CMMI includes ways to get your organization to focus on defining and following its processes. Through training and standardization, you can make sure all members of the organization know their roles and understand how to execute them in the process. The measurement data you collect can be applied to improve your process performance, to innovate when processes need to evolve, and to ensure that your organization is able to meet changing needs.

Processes need to be planned just like projects, and it helps if the organization has given some weight and validity to process compliance through policy. You need to make sure that resources are available for trained, empowered people to perform the process. Those with a vested interest in a process need to be identified and involved. Work products that result from performing a process should be managed, the process documentation should be controlled, and progress against the process plan should be tracked as well. Someone should be responsible for objectively evaluating that the process is being followed, and management should be briefed periodically on process performance.

Processes become more capable when they are standardized across the organization and their performance is monitored against historical data. With capable processes, you can detect variations in performance and address potential problems early. Ultimately, you should be continuously improving the processes by identifying the root causes of process variability and finding innovative ways to make them better.

3.1.3 CMMI and Business Objectives

In Chapter 1, we identified some common organizational business objectives. Based on this brief overview of CMMI's process content and concern with process improvement, how could you expect CMMI to help your organization in meeting such objectives? Let's look at each objective individually.

Produce Quality Products or Services. The process improvement concept in CMMI models evolved from the Deming, Juran, and Crosby quality paradigm: Quality products are a result of quality processes. CMMI has a strong focus on quality-related activities, including requirements management, quality assurance, verification, and validation.

Create Value for the Stockholders. Mature organizations are likely to make better cost and revenue estimates than those with less maturity, and then exhibit performance in line with those estimates. CMMI supports quality products, predictable schedules, and effective measures to support management in making accurate and defensible forecasts. Process maturity can guard against project performance problems that could weaken the value of the organization in the eyes of investors.

Be an Employer of Choice. Watts Humphrey has said, "Quality work is not done by accident; it is done only by skilled and motivated people."[1] CMMI emphasizes training, both in disciplines and in process. Experience has shown that organizations with mature processes have far less turnover than immature organizations. Engineers, in particular, are more comfortable in an organization where there is a sense of cohesion and competence.

Enhance Customer Satisfaction. Meeting cost and schedule targets with high-quality products that are validated against customer needs is a good formula for customer satisfaction. CMMI addresses all of these

---

1. Humphrey, W. *Winning with Software.* Boston: Addison-Wesley, 2002.

ingredients through its emphasis on planning, monitoring, and measuring, and the improved predictability that comes with more capable processes.

Increase Market Share. Market share is a result of many factors, including quality products and services, name identification, pricing, and image. Clearly customer satisfaction is a central factor, and in the marketplace having satisfied customers can be contagious. Customers like to deal with suppliers that have a reputation for meeting their commitments. CMMI improves estimation and lowers process variability to enable better, more accurate bids that are demonstrably achievable. It also contributes to meeting essential quality goals.

Implement Cost Savings and Successful Practices. CMMI encourages measurement as a managerial tool. By using the historical data collected to support project estimation, an organization can identify and widely deploy practices that work, and eliminate those that don't.

Gain an Industry-wide Recognition for Excellence. The best way to develop a reputation for excellence is to consistently perform well on projects, delivering quality products and services that address user needs within cost and schedule parameters. Having processes that incorporate CMMI practices can enhance that reputation.

As you can see, CMMI comprises information that can make a significant impact on your organization and on the achievement of your business objectives. In the next sections, we'll discuss a different set of objectives—those that led to the development of CMMI itself. In addition, we explore the models that were used as the basis for the information CMMI contains, and something of the structure in place to manage it. More detail on CMMI contents is provided in subsequent chapters.

3.2 CMMI Objectives

While CMMI has many business-related benefits, the CMMI project as defined by its sponsors was directed toward the development of more efficient and effective process improvement models. It had both initial and longer-term objectives. The initial objective (represented in version 1.1 of the CMMI Product Suite) was to integrate three specific process improvement models: software, systems engineering, and integrated product and process development. This integration was intended to reduce the cost of implementing multidisciplinary model-based process improvement by accomplishing the following tasks:

- Eliminating inconsistencies
- Reducing duplication
- Increasing clarity and understanding
- Providing common terminology
- Providing consistent style
- Establishing uniform construction rules
- Maintaining common components
- Assuring consistency with ISO/IEC 15504

In the update to CMMI version 1.2, one objective of the CMMI Team was to improve and simplify the model as it applies to engineering development activities.[2] A second objective was to expand the scope of the model beyond the world of development to include both acquisition and the delivery of services.[3] Figure 3-1 illustrates these objectives and the product line approach developed by the CMMI Team. It remains to be seen whether in the future other disciplines and constellations[4] will be added to the CMMI Product Suite.

To facilitate both current and future model integration, the CMMI Team created an automated, extensible framework that can house model components, training material components, and appraisal materials. Defined rules govern the potential addition of more disciplines into this framework.

From the start, the CMMI project had to find an acceptable balance between competing requirements relating to change. The task of integration, which by its very nature requires change from each of the original single-discipline models, meant that all model users could expect new ways of thinking about process improvement to be needed in a CMMI environment. At the same time, an equally strong requirement called for protecting the investments in process improvement made by

---

2. The "CMMI Team" encompasses all who were and are involved in the CMMI project, including the Steering Group, the Product Team, and the Stakeholder Group. See Section 3.4 for a description of the CMMI Project Organization.

3. CMMI-DEV designates the CMMI model constellation that addresses development activities, and with the addition of IPPD included the designation becomes CMMI-DEV +IPPD; CMMI-ACQ designates the model constellation as it applies to acquisition organizations; and CMMI-SVC designates the model constellation (still being developed as we go to publication with this book) as it applies to service providers.

4. A constellation groups together the parts of the model that apply to a special area of interest.

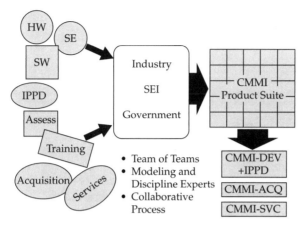

Figure 3-1: *The CMMI concept*

CMMI Milestones

1997	CMMI initiated by U.S. Department of Defense and NDIA
1998	First team meeting held
1999	Concept of operations released
	First pilot completed
2000	Additional pilots completed
	CMMI-SE/SW version 1.0 released for initial use
	CMMI-SE/SW/IPPD version 1.0 released for initial use
	CMMI-SE/SW/IPPD/SS released for piloting
2002	CMMI-SE/SW version 1.1 released
	CMMI-SE/SW/IPPD version 1.1 released
	CMMI-SE/SW/IPPD/SS version 1.1 released
	CMMI-SW version 1.1 released
2006	CMMI-DEV version 1.2 released
	CMMI-DEV +IPPD version 1.2 released
2007	CMMI-ACQ version 1.2 released

former users of those models, which meant controlling the introduction of new materials for each discipline. Judging from the significant rate of adoption throughout the world, we believe the CMMI project has achieved an appropriate balance between old and new.

3.3 The Three Source Models

To truly appreciate the significance of the CMMI accomplishments, you need to understand a bit of the history that led up to the development of the CMMI product suite. Of primary importance are the stories of the source models. Table 3-1 summarizes the three source models for CMMI.

Table 3-1: *Source Models for CMMI*

Model Discipline	*Source Model*
Software	SW-CMM, draft version 2(c)
Systems Engineering	EIA/IS 731
Integrated Product and Process Development	IPD-CMM, version 0.98

3.3.1 The CMM for Software

The character of software development sometimes seems closer to mathematics and art than it does to most other engineering disciplines. Software is inherently an intangible, intellectual development medium. No laws of physics govern its behavior; it is both marvelously and dangerously malleable. For this reason, it is critical that mature disciplines and processes be applied when working with software.

Software engineering and process management have been intimately associated since the pioneering work of Ron Radice and Richard Phillips in Watts Humphrey's group at IBM in the 1980s.[5] Basing their work on the tenets of the quality movement, Radice and Phillips led the

---

5. Radice, R. A., and R. W. Phillips. *Software Engineering, an Industrial Approach* (Vol. 1). Englewood Cliffs, NJ: Prentice Hall, 1988; Radice, R. A., J. T. Harding, P. E. Munnis, and R. W. Philips. A Programming Process Study. *IBM System Journals*, 2/3, 1999.

way in crafting a way to capture successful software development practices and then organize those practices so as to help struggling organizations get a handle on their processes and improve them. Given the nature of software development, it was not surprising that the large majority of the practices related to management discipline and processes.

Software Engineering

As defined in IEEE Standard 610.12, *software engineering* is the application of a systematic, disciplined, quantifiable approach to the development, operation, and maintenance of software—that is, the application of engineering to software.[6]

In 1986, Watts Humphrey, the SEI, and the Mitre Corporation responded to a request by the U.S. federal government to create a way of evaluating the software capability of its contractors. The group used IBM's concepts to create a software maturity framework, a questionnaire, and two appraisal methods. Over the next few years, this work was continued and refined.

In 1991, the SEI published the CMM for Software version 1.0, a model that describes the principles and practices underlying software process maturity. The CMM is organized to help software organizations improve along an evolutionary path, growing from an ad hoc, chaotic environment into mature, disciplined software processes. The CMM was used and evaluated for two years, and then revised and released as version 1.1 in 1993.[7] A similar revision was planned for 1997 as version 2.0;[8] this version was developed but never released as an independent model. However, the good work did not go to waste: The proposed revision was used as the source for the CMMI integration effort. In addition, two documents regarding software appraisals were used: the CMM

---

6. *IEEE Standard Glossary of Software Engineering Terminology.* IEEE Standard 610.12–1990. New York: Institute of Electrical and Electronics Engineers, 1990.

7. Paulk, Mark C., et al. *Capability Maturity Model for Software, Version 1.1.* CMU/SEI-93-TR-24; also ESC-TR-93-177. Pittsburgh, PA: Software Engineering Institute, Carnegie Mellon University, February 1993; Paulk, M., et al. *The Capability Maturity Model: Guidelines for Improving the Software Process.* Boston: Addison Wesley, 1995.

8. For more on the history of the CMM for Software, see Paulk, Mark C. The Evolution of the SEI's Capability Maturity Model for Software. *Software Process—Improvement and Practice,* 1995, 3–15.

Appraisal Framework, version 1.0,[9] and the CMM-Based Appraisal for Internal Process Improvement (CBA IPI): Method Description.[10]

Software engineering's scope extends beyond the primary material contained in the CMM for Software to include software-related topics such as requirements elicitation, installation, operation, and maintenance. The CMMI model covers these areas in more detail through inclusion of appropriate material from the Systems Engineering Capability Model.

3.3.2 The Systems Engineering Capability Model

Systems engineering integrates all of the system-related disciplines so that systems meet business and technical needs in the most effective way, while striving to minimize local optimization and maximize return on investment. Another way of envisioning systems engineering is as the application of a set of rigorous engineering techniques to the solution of a complex technical problem.

> ### Systems Engineering
>
> INCOSE defines *systems engineering* as "an interdisciplinary approach and means to enable the realization of successful systems."[11]

It is difficult to fully understand the scope of systems engineering without looking at the various specialty disciplines associated with it. In *Essentials of Project and Systems Engineering Management*, Howard Eisner lists 30 key elements of systems engineering. These elements include such diverse areas as mission engineering, architectural design, life-cycle costing, alternatives analysis, technical data management, operations and maintenance, integrated logistics support, and reengineering.[12]

The systems engineering material in the CMMI has a complex history. In a modern-day "Tale of Two Capability Models," two organizations

---

9. Masters, S., and C. Bothwell. *CMM Appraisal Framework (CMU/SEI-95-TR-001)*. Pittsburgh, PA: Software Engineering Institute, Carnegie Mellon University, February 1995.

10. Dunaway, D., and S. Masters. *CMM-Based Appraisal for Internal Process Improvement (CBA IPI): Method Description (CMU/SEI-96-TR-007)*. Pittsburgh, PA: Software Engineering Institute, Carnegie Mellon University, April 1996.

11. INCOSE Winter Workshop, January 1996.

12. Eisner, Howard. *Essentials of Project and Systems Engineering Management*. New York: Wiley Interscience, 1997.

undertook to model systems engineering practices. In August 1995, the Enterprise Process Improvement Collaboration (EPIC—a group of industry, academic, and government organizations) released the Systems Engineering Capability Maturity Model (SE-CMM). EPIC enlisted the SEI and architect Roger Bate to lead the development. The team pulled its systems engineering expertise primarily from aerospace and defense industry corporations and from the Software Productivity Consortium. The result was a model based on the appraisal model architecture contained in draft versions of ISO/IEC 15504 that addressed engineering, project, process, and organization practices.[13]

Around the same time that the SE-CMM was under development, INCOSE created a checklist for evaluating the capabilities of systems engineering organizations based on various engineering standards. Over time, this checklist evolved into a full-blown capability model known as the Systems Engineering Capability Assessment Model (SECAM). SECAM extended the SPICE concepts of a continuous model but focused more specifically on systems engineering practices than the SE-CMM, using EIA 632, "Processes for Engineering a Model," as the fundamental reference.

Needless to say, an environment with two models developed by two reputable organizations that purported to address the same issues was ripe for a model war. Which model would emerge as the "standard" by which organizations could be evaluated? After a year of heated discussions, in 1996 EPIC and INCOSE agreed to work together under the auspices of the Government Electronic and Information Technology Association (GEIA) of the Electronic Industries Alliance (EIA), with the goal of merging the two models into a single EIA standard. The result was an interim standard EIA/IS 731, "Systems Engineering Capability Model" (SECM).[14] By issuing the interim standard, the systems engineering community could apply a single, common description of systems engineering processes to the CMMI project.

---

13. In January 1993, an international working group (WG 10) was formed as part of subcommittee 7 (SC7) of the ISO/IEC Joint Technical Committee 1 (JTC1) to create a standard for software process assessment. Piloting of working drafts was accomplished through a project called SPICE (Software Process Improvement and Capability dEtermination). The combined effort of WG 10 and the SPICE project resulted in the development of ISO/IEC 15504 as a draft standard. At the time of writing the third edition of this book, an international standard has been released, and it has been refocused to address "process assessment" generally—that is, it is not limited just to software process assessment.

14. *EIA Interim Standard, Systems Engineering Capability*. EIA/IS 731 (Part 1: Model, EIA/IS 731–1, version 1.0; Part 2: Appraisal Method, EIA/IS 731–2, version 1.0), 1999. This was converted to a full standard, EIA 731, in 2002.

Systems engineering in CMMI remains heavily influenced by EIA 731. While echoes of the controversy between SECM and SE-CMM found voice in CMMI discussions, the resulting systems engineering content reflects an even stronger evolution of the original concepts. It preserves some of the innovations of EIA 731 while providing a more consistent underlying architecture compatible with the emerging international standards.[15] The standard includes both the SECM model (Part 1) and an appraisal method (Part 2).

3.3.3 The Integrated Product Development CMM

The source model for integrated product and process development was a draft of the Integrated Product Development CMM, known as IPD CMM version 0.98. This model had been developed almost to the point of its initial formal release when the CMMI project began in 1998.

From the outset, the CMMI Team wanted to include the concept of integrated product and process development (IPPD) in the CMMI product suite. This concept was fundamental to many of the large member corporations of NDIA, and it was strongly supported by the Department of Defense (DoD).[16] Unfortunately, the definition of IPPD used in the CMMI requirements document was derived from the DoD's experience with integrated operation of government system acquisition programs—and acquisition was not an initial discipline for CMMI. This discrepancy led to some difficulty in addressing the IPPD tenets within the CMMI scope. Adding to the confusion was a lack of consensus in the industry (and among members of the CMMI Team) regarding the fundamental concepts and best practices of integrated product development. Because it represented a relatively new means of organizing and accomplishing engineering work, there were nearly as many definitions as there were organizations.

This problem was not unique to CMMI. Indeed, the team established by EPIC to develop the IPD CMM, which was supported by many of the same members of the SE-CMM team, struggled with IPPD concepts for more than two years before being subsumed into the CMMI effort. The final draft IPD-CMM was established as a source document for CMMI, but the draft never achieved the status of a finished product.

---

15. For example, see ISO/IEC 15504 and ISO/IEC 15288.
16. The U.S. Air Force played a significant role in the development of the IPD CMM.

> ### *Integrated Product and Process Development*
>
> CMMI defines *integrated product and process development* as a systematic approach to product development that achieves a timely collaboration of necessary disciplines throughout the product life cycle, to better satisfy customer needs, expectations, and requirements.

IPPD emphasizes the involvement of stakeholders from all technical and business functions throughout the product development life cycle—customers, suppliers, and developers of both the product and product-related processes, such as testing and evaluation, manufacturing, support, training, marketing, purchasing, financial, contracting, and disposal processes. Clearly, implementing IPPD affects more than an organization's engineering processes and practices. Because it is essentially a way of doing business, it may radically change organizational structure and modify leadership behavior.

3.4 CMMI Project Organization

During the development phase that led to the initial CMMI materials, the project was organized in terms of a Steering Group, a Product Development Team, and a Stakeholder Group. In all, it involved the efforts of more than 200 people over a period of more than six years. The three groups comprised representatives from industry, government, and the SEI. Representatives of the disciplines whose models were to be integrated into CMMI were included in all three groups.

The Steering Group produced a list of requirements for CMMI, which was then reviewed by the Stakeholder Group and subsequently used by the Product Development Team to guide its creation of the CMMI products. The Product Development Team was a cross-disciplinary group created for the initial development work; it was charged with ensuring that the viewpoints and interests of each discipline were adequately considered in the integration process. The Stakeholder Group reviewed the initial draft CMMI materials, with its work being followed by a public review of a second round of draft materials, prior to the release of version 1.0 in late 2000. Taking advantage of early feedback from version 1.0 users, and responding to more than 1500 change requests, version 1.1 of the Product Suite was released in 2002.

The CMMI Team

The following organizations supplied members to the CMMI Team: ADP Inc., Aerospace Corp., AT&T Labs, BAE Systems, Boeing, CIBIT, Comarco Sys., Computer Sciences Corp., EDS, EER Sys., Ericsson Canada, Ernst and Young, General Dynamics, General Motors, Harris Corp., Hewlett-Packard, Honeywell, IBM, INCOSE, Institute for Defense Analyses, Integrated System Diagnostics, Jacobs Engineering, JPMorganChase, KPMG Consulting, Lockheed Martin, MitoKen Solutions, MITRE Corp., Motorola, NASA, Norimatsu Process Engineering Lab., Northrop Grumman, Pacific Bell, Q-Labs, Raytheon, Rockwell Collins, SAIC, SEI, Siemens, Spirula, SRA, SSCI, TeraQuest, THALES, U.S. DAU, U.S. DCMA, U.S. DLA, U.S. DoD, U.S. DHS, U.S. FAA, U.S. GAO, U.S. MDA, U.S. NRO, U.S. NSA, U.S. Air Force, U.S. Army, U.S. Navy, and Wibas.

The cross-disciplinary team that produced the initial CMMI models included members with backgrounds in software engineering, systems engineering, and integrated product and process development. Most engineering organizations maintain these skills, but the manner in which they are aligned and interact varies across organizations. Thus the CMMI Team not only had to resolve differences between the three source models, but also had to bridge the cultural, linguistic, and professional differences separating engineering specialties and organizations. The bridges that had to be built in constructing the CMMI models serve as precursors of those that users of the models will need to construct to successfully support integrated process improvement and process appraisal.

During the CMMI development effort, the CMMI Team actively sought to keep balanced membership across the three disciplines. This move was supported by the strong interest espoused by the software and systems engineering communities. Thanks to the wide acceptance of the

CMM Software, strong advocacy was provided by the SEI and organizations that had used the model, understood its value, and wanted to see that value preserved in the integrated CMMI models. Likewise, in the systems engineering world, the International Council on Systems Engineering (INCOSE) advocated inclusion of systems engineering practices. Even the integrated product and process development community was represented on the CMMI Team, albeit with members voicing a somewhat wider range of views on how integrated product and process development should be handled than did the more established discipline representatives. In the end, this team of experienced and active people, each of whom brought his or her specific expertise and preferences to the table, came together to create the CMMI product suite.

Once the development phase of the initial CMMI product suite was complete, a new organizational structure was established (see Figure 3-2). That is, the CMMI Team evolved into the CMMI Product Team that exists today. This team has access to expert groups for software, systems engineering, integrated product and process development,

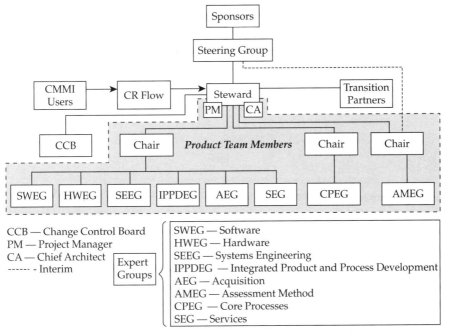

Figure 3-2: *Current CMMI project organization*

supplier sourcing, appraisals, and the core CMMI components. A configuration control board was established to guide CMMI evolution, and the SEI was named as the Steward of the CMMI Product Suite. In its role as Steward, SEI is responsible for maintenance and support of CMMI. As time goes on, new cross-functional teams of experts will be required to handle revisions of existing products and the subsequent work of adding disciplines to the CMMI framework such as the Services Constellation Team and the Acquisition Constellation Team.

Chapter 4

CMMI Content

All that is gold does not glitter,
Not all who wander are lost.
J. R. R. Tolkien, *The Fellowship of the Ring* (1954)

I have gathered a posie of other men's flowers,
and nothing but the thread that binds them is mine own.
John Bartlett, Preface to *Familiar Quotations* (1901)

What's in a Capability Maturity Model Integration (CMMI) model, and how can your organization use it? At several hundred pages in length, the CMMI models seem formidable to even the most experienced process improvement champion. With just a little understanding of how the models are put together and what kind of material is presented, however, you can begin to navigate the depths of CMMI with confidence. This chapter describes the types of information you can find in the CMMI models and notes the location where you can find it. You will also learn to interpret the importance of the various types of information.

4.1 Constellations

Constellations provide a way for the CMMI to be used, with as much commonality as possible, for different types of organizations.[1] The two constellations in CMMI version 1.2 are Development and Acquisition; material for a possible third constellation for Services is being created. The Development constellation supports organizations that develop products and is the successor to all of the previous versions of CMMI. The Acquisition constellation supports an organization in procuring products or services from suppliers outside of the organization. The Services constellation is intended to support organizations that primarily deliver services rather than products. The CMMI Framework provides the information necessary to produce the different models. Here we introduce the architecture and use of the CMMI Framework.[2]

Constellations are actually a part of the CMMI Framework: A collection of components used to construct CMMI models, CMMI training materials, and CMMI appraisal methods. A key part of the CMMI Framework is the CMMI Model Foundation (CMF), which consists of material common to every existing and future CMMI model. The model components include process areas, goals, practices, and informative material about the use of the model. The model components are described in the following sections of this chapter, and the CMF is described more fully in Chapter 7.

4.2 Process Areas

The fundamental organizational feature of all the CMMI models is the "process area." Not everything related to processes and process improvement is included in a process improvement model. Like its

---

1. The term "constellation" is an element of the CMMI architecture that is used to characterize parts of the model that work together to address improvement in specific areas of interest. (Definition: A *constellation* is a collection of components that are used to construct models, training material, and appraisal materials in an area of interest.) There is some uncertainty whether in the future this architectural construct and this term will continue to be used. The authors make use of the current architecture and terminology for this edition of the book, but readers should be aware that this situation may change in the future.
2. A Technical Note from the SEI describes the CMMI Framework, the CMMI Model Foundation, and the Structure of CMMI Models. See *Introduction to the Architecture of the CMMI Framework*, CMU/SEI-2007-TN-009.

predecessor models, CMMI selects only the most important topics for process improvement and then groups those topics into "areas." The number of process areas varies with each constellation.

We will discuss the CMMI process areas in detail in Chapter 7. For now, to introduce the concept of a process area, let's look at one and see what it covers. For our example, we'll use Requirements Management.

Within systems, software, and hardware engineering, it is widely believed that the management of the product requirements is a central area of concern during any development effort. Experience has demonstrated that failure to adequately identify the requirements and manage changes to them is a major cause of projects not meeting their cost, schedule, or quality objectives. This experience justifies collecting information related to the management of requirements into a major model component—that is, a process area. Users of the model should, therefore, focus on this process area to establish capability relating to the management of requirements.

As stated in the model, the *purpose* of the Requirements Management process area is "to manage the requirements of the project's products and product components and to identify inconsistencies between those requirements and the project's plans and work products." In addition to this purpose, the process area has *goals* that describe the results of a successful requirements management process and *practices* that can help achieve these goals. A great deal of explanatory and "how to" material is also supplied to provide some concrete help with managing requirements. That's pretty much a process area in a nutshell.

4.3 Content Classification

Any process improvement model must, of necessity, indicate the importance and role of the materials contained in the model. In the CMMI models, a distinction is drawn between the terms "required," "expected," and "informative." The most important material is *required;* these items are essential to the model and to an understanding of what is needed for process improvement and demonstrations of conformance to the model. Second in importance is the *expected* material; these items may not be essential, and in some instances they may not be present in an organization that successfully uses the model. Nevertheless, expected material is presumed to play a central role in process improvement; such items are a strong indicator that the required components are being achieved. Third in importance (and largest in quantity) is *informative* material; these items constitute the majority of the model. The informative material provides useful guidance for process improvement, and in many instances it may offer clarification regarding the intended meaning of the required and expected components.

If you are seeking only a quick overview of a CMMI model, one recommended approach is to review all of the required material. This strategy may be thought of as an "executive overview" level. For a medium-level review, you could focus on the combined required and expected materials. This approach may be considered a "manager overview" level. With either type of review, the best place to look is in the model summary in Appendix A of this book. Here the first two categories of model components are joined (with a very minimal amount of informative material) to present only the most essential elements of the model.

4.4 Required Materials

The sole required component of the CMMI models is the "goal." A goal represents a desirable end state, the achievement of which indicates that a certain degree of project and process control has been achieved. When a goal is unique to a single process area, it is called a "specific goal." In contrast, when a goal may apply across all of the process areas, it is called a "generic goal." Table 4-1 lists four examples of specific goals. Each process area has between one and four specific goals; the entire CMMI for Development version 1.2 model includes a total of 50 specific goals.

As is evident from the four examples in Table 4-1, a goal statement is fairly succinct. Reviewing the expected and informative materials in the process area can help you to understand the specific goal in practical terms.

In contrast to a specific goal, a generic goal has a scope that crosses all of the process areas. Because their application is so broad, the wording of generic goals is more abstract than the wording of specific goals. Consider, for example, GG 2: "The process is institutionalized as a managed process." To better understand what this statement means,

Table 4-1: *Specific Goals for Four Process Areas*

Process Area	Specific Goal
Requirements Management	REQM SG 1: Requirements are managed and inconsistencies with project plans and work products are identified.
Project Monitoring and Control	PMC SG 2: Corrective actions are managed to closure when the project's performance or results deviate significantly from the plan.
Organizational Process Performance	OPP SG 1: Baselines and models that characterize the expected process performance of the organization's set of standard processes are established and maintained.
Causal Analysis and Resolution	CAR SG 2: Root causes of defects and other problems are systematically addressed to prevent their future occurrence.

let's start with the CMMI Glossary (CMMI for Development version 1.2, Appendix D). There we find the definition of "institutionalization" and "managed process." Both definitions are provided in Table 4-2.

Taken together, these two definitions provide much more detail than the short statement of the generic goal itself. Nevertheless, even with these definitions, questions about practical meaning may linger. What are the key features of the "ingrained way of doing business"? How is a process "evaluated for adherence to process description"?

Although the goal is the only required component in a CMMI model, no statement of any goal—specific or generic—can be fully understood without exploring more of the model. The first expansion of that understanding comes by looking at the expected components.

Table 4-2: *Definitions Related to CMMI Generic Goal 2*

CMMI Glossary Term	CMMI Definition
Institutionalization	The ingrained way of doing business that an organization follows routinely as part of its corporate culture.
Managed process	A "managed process" is a performed process that is planned and executed in accordance with policy; employs skilled people having adequate resources to produce controlled outputs; involves relevant stakeholders; is monitored, controlled, and reviewed; and is evaluated for adherence to its process description.

4.5 Expected Materials

The sole expected component of the CMMI models is a "practice." A set of practices represent the "expected" means of achieving a goal. Every practice in the CMMI model is mapped to exactly one goal. A practice is not a required component, however; an organization may achieve a goal in a way that does not rely on the performance of all the practices that are mapped to that goal. That is, "alternative" practices may provide an equally useful way of reaching the goal. It may help to think of the practices as critical success factors; if you aren't addressing them, understanding their absence is important.

When a practice is unique to a single process area, it is called a "specific practice." When a practice may apply across all of the process areas, it is called a "generic practice."

Table 4-3 details several examples of specific practices, together with the specific goals to which they are mapped. Note that a goal, which represents an end state, is always written in the passive voice, whereas a practice, as a means to achieve the goal, is always written in the active voice.

Between two and seven specific practices are mapped to each specific goal; the entire CMMI for Development version 1.2 model includes a total of 173 specific practices, which are mapped to the 50 specific goals.

Table 4-3: *Specific Practices Associated with Specific Goals*

Specific Goal	Specific Practice
REQM SG 1: Requirements are managed and inconsistencies with project plans and work products are identified.	REQM SP 1.1: Develop an understanding with the requirements providers on the meaning of the requirements.
PMC SG 2: Corrective actions are managed to closure when the project's performance or results deviate significantly from the plan.	PMC SP 2.1: Collect and analyze the issues and determine the corrective actions necessary to address the issues.
OPP SG 1: Baselines and models that characterize the expected process performance of the organization's set of standard processes are established and maintained.	OPP SP 1.2: Establish and maintain definitions of the measures that are to be included in the organization's process performance analyses.
CAR SG 2: Root causes of defects and other problems are systematically addressed to prevent their future occurrence.	CAR SP 2.2: Evaluate the effect of changes on process performance.

When the specific practices mapped to a specific goal are taken as a unit, they provide additional insight into how the goal should be understood. Table 4-4 shows one specific goal with its full complement of specific practices. In this example, establishing and maintaining work-product baselines involves identifying configuration items, implementing a configuration and change management system, and establishing baselines for both internal and external use.

In contrast to a specific practice, a generic practice has a scope that crosses all of the process areas. For example, one generic practice that is mapped to the generic goal to institutionalize a managed process (GG 2) addresses the training of people. Consider GP 2.5: "Train the people performing or supporting the process as needed." In other words, a project is expected to provide the training that is needed when it follows a

Table 4-4: *Specific Goal and Specific Practices for Configuration Management*

Specific Goal	Specific Practices
Configuration Management (CM) SG 1: Baselines of identified work products are established.	CM SP 1.1: Identify the configuration items, components, and related work products that will be placed under configuration-management. CM SP 1.2: Establish and maintain a configuration management and change management system for controlling work products. CM SP 1.3: Create or release baselines for internal use and for delivery to the customer.

managed process in such a way that the process becomes institutionalized. For each process area in a CMMI model, needed training is expected based on the application of this generic practice.

4.6 Informative Materials

CMMI models may contain as many as 10 types of informative components, taken from the following list.[3]

1. Purpose. Each process area begins with a brief statement of purpose for the process area. Generally, a purpose statement consists of one or two sentences that summarize or draw together the specific goals of the process area. Consider the purpose statement from Risk Management:

> *The purpose of Risk Management is to identify potential problems before they occur, so that risk-handling activities can be planned and invoked as needed across the life of the product or project to mitigate adverse impacts on achieving objectives.*

---

3. Not all models make use of each of the informative components. For example, the CMMI-DEV does not use Typical Supplier Deliverables and the CMMI-ACQ does not use either Generic Practice Elaborations or Discipline Amplifications. So while there are 11 types of informative components, currently no model uses more than 10.

The three specific goals in Risk Management address preparations, identification and analysis of risk, and mitigation as needed. In this way, the purpose statement provides a quick, high-level orientation for the entire process area.

2. Introductory Note. A section including multiple introductory notes that apply to the entire process area follows the purpose statement. Typically, these notes present information on the scope of the process area, its importance, the way in which it reflects recognized successful practices, unique terminology used in it, and the interaction of it with other process areas.

3. Reference. Explicit pointing from one process area to all or part of another process area is accomplished with a reference. In CMMI, a reference is simply an indicator noting that, to obtain more information on some topic, one should look in another process area.

4. Names. In CMMI, all required and expected components (goals and practices) are given a name, which provides a convenient handle for referring to the component. Table 4-5 lists examples of names from the Measurement and Analysis (MA) process area. Thus, in training classes or in discussion, we can refer to the "align activities" goal or the "specify measures" practice in Measurement and Analysis. Although this name provides a convenient shorthand, do not confuse the name of the model component with the component itself. The components form the basis for process improvement and process appraisal—not the names.

5. Specific Goal and Practice Summary. Using the names for goals and practices, the relationship table in each process area maps each specific and generic practice to its related specific or generic goal, respectively.

Table 4-5: *Names from the Measurement and Analysis Process Area*

Component	Name	Required or Expected Material
MA SG 1	Align Measurement and Analysis Activities	Measurement objectives and activities are aligned with identified information needs and objectives.
MA SP 1.2	Specify Measures	Specify measures to address the measurement objectives.

6. Notes. Whereas the general notes at the beginning of a process area are labeled as "introductory notes," there are also (plain) notes attached to other model components, such as goals, practices, and subpractices. These notes represent a rich source of information that should prove valuable in planning and conducting process improvement efforts. In the model, examples are highlighted by a box outlining the note.

7. Typical Work Products. When a practice is performed, there will often be outputs in the form of work products. In the Glossary, a work product is defined (in part) as follows:

> *Sample outputs from a specific practice. These examples are called typical work products because there are often other work products that are just as effective but are not listed.*

These work products can include files, documents, parts of the product, services, process descriptions, and specifications.

The items identified in a list of typical work products are examples; they should not be considered essential to the performance of the process, and the list should not be thought of as exhaustive. The intention is merely to provide initial guidance regarding the type of work products that may be produced by a practice. During an appraisal, however, you will be required to produce evidence proving that your process produces outputs and to show examples of those outputs to get credit for institutionalization of the process area.

8. Typical Supplier Deliverables. These components are used only in the CMMI for Acquisition model. A typical supplier deliverable represents an artifact that is input into or supports the acquirer's implementation of the practice.

9. Subpractices. For many practices in the CMMI models, subpractices provide a decomposition of their meaning and the activities that they might entail as well as an elaboration of their use. Unlike practices, which are expected model components, subpractices appear in the model for information purposes only.

10. Discipline Amplifications. One of the most distinctive aspects of CMMI as compared with prior source models is the fact that the CMMI model components are discipline independent. The advantage of this approach derives from the ability of different disciplines to use the same components, which promotes common terminology and understanding across various disciplines. The limitation on discipline-independent components becomes apparent, however, when one considers that generalization can entail the removal of content. For example, the CMM Software included a practice that made explicit reference to developing estimates of software size. In contrast, CMMI speaks more generally about producing estimates for the attributes of work products and tasks (see Project Planning, SP 1.2–1).

To maintain the usefulness of the discipline-specific material found in its source models, CMMI provides discipline amplifications that are introduced with phrases such as "For Hardware Engineering," "For Software Engineering," or "For Systems Engineering." For example, in the Project Planning process area, the specific practice on establishing the project plan has a discipline amplification for software that mentions the common names of software plans. It also has a discipline amplification for hardware engineering that mentions the hardware development plan and addresses production plans. Amplifications are informative material, so they are not required in an appraisal. Nevertheless, the appraisers may use them as guidance on how to interpret the practice for specific disciplines and to gain a better idea of how the practice will affect the process improvement activities.

11. *Generic Practice Elaborations.* Whereas discipline amplifications provide details for each specific discipline, generic practice elaborations provide details regarding the application of a generic practice in a given process area. For example, in the Product Integration process area, an elaboration of the generic practice on establishing an organizational policy is explained with these words:

> *This policy establishes organizational expectations for developing product integration sequences, procedures, and an environment, ensuring interface compatibility among product components, assembling the product components, and delivering the product and product components.*

Sometimes, in a given process area, a generic practice and a specific practice may seem to address a similar topic. For example, the generic practice may deal with planning the process, and a specific practice may focus on planning a particular aspect of the process. In such a circumstance, a generic practice elaboration is used to comment on the distinction intended between the generic and specific practices.

4.7 Additions

Additions extend the scope of a model or emphasize a particular aspect of its use. They can be additional process areas, specific goals, specific practices, or informative material. In CMMI for Development version 1.2, the only additions that exist are related to IPPD. An example IPPD Addition can be found in Organizational Process Definition +IPPD, GP 2.6:

Examples of work products placed under control include the following:

- Empowerment rules and guidelines for people and integrated teams
- Organizational process documentation for issue resolution

The CMMI for Services constellation currently has three additions. Each one is a complete process area. See Chapter 7 for a discussion of the CMMI-SVC.

4.8 CMMI Model Foundation

Earlier in this chapter we mentioned the CMF but did not explain its significance in the CMMI Framework. This section describes how the CMF is used.

The CMF contains components that must be used in every constellation. However, constellation-specific information can be added to the CMF. For example, the notes associated with a practice can be marked as CMF material. The CMF notes cannot be modified in any way, but a new note can be added to a practice to clarify some aspect of the practice within the constellation. In fact, material associated with any process area component can be added to a CMF process area, including specific goals, specific practices, and any informative component.

Each constellation comprises a collection of process areas (see Section 4.2). The CMF contains the 16 core process areas that are common to all constellations:

Causal Analysis and Resolution

Configuration Management

Decision Analysis and Resolution

Integrated Project Management

Measurement and Analysis

Organizational Innovation and Deployment

Organizational Process Definition

Organizational Process Focus

Organizational Process Performance

Organizational Training

Project Monitoring and Control

Project Planning

Process and Product Quality Assurance

Quantitative Project Management

Requirements Management

Risk Management

Each constellation is composed of the following elements:

- The CMF
- Named groups of non-CMF materials to expand the scope of the CMF in various ways[4]
- Generic practice elaborations [See Section 4.6(11)] for the process areas in the constellation (optional)
- Appropriate training materials
- Appraisal materials

The models of a constellation are constructed by inserting selected non-CMF materials including amplifications into the CMF, and optionally inserting the generic practice elaborations for the process areas into the model.

4.9 Document Map

Figure 4-1 shows where to find the various types of information described in this chapter. The illustration is from the downloadable model.[5]

---

4. For example, non-CMF materials in CMMI-DEV include all of the Engineering process areas. An IPPD group of additions consisting of specific goals to be added to IPM and OPF creates the CMMI-DEV +IPPD model.

5. The model is formatted differently in the book *CMMI: Guidelines for Process Integration and Product Improvement*. See Section 5.4 for more information.

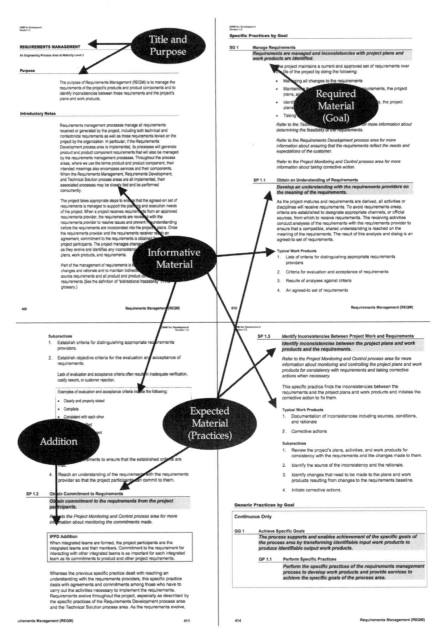

Figure 4-1: *Document map for the model*

Chapter 5

CMMI Representations

If we cannot now end our differences,
at least we can help make the world safe for diversity.
John Fitzgerald Kennedy (1963)

We tend to see our own experiences as the normal process,
so we are often amazed that anyone could have taken a different path.
But when we do meet up, it's always fascinating to compare notes about the
different ways to get there.
Daniel Gilly, *Unix in a Nutshell* (1992)

In previous versions of the CMMI models, the user faced a fundamental choice: Do you use the continuous representation or the staged representation? In fact, a distinct, separately published representation was available for each of these options—one for continuous and one for staged. CMMI version 1.2 brings these two representations closer together. For example, advanced practices[1] and common features,[2]

---

1. In the continuous representation of CMMI V1.1, advanced practices were specific practices that resided at capability levels 2 and 3. They were located in the Engineering process areas only.
2. In the staged representation of CMMI V1.1, common features provided four groups of generic practices: commitment to perform, ability to perform, directing implementation, and verifying implementation.

both of which were in the earlier model versions, have been removed. Also, in version 1.2 a single published model contains both representations. However, one architectural feature remains that makes the two representations different: the use of generic goals and practices.[3]

The two representations exist in CMMI to provide users with multiple tools for process improvement. The key to using the model is to follow a structured approach for process improvement, and multiple ways to do this are provided. In this chapter, we address how different approaches to process improvement relate to continuous and staged representations.

An organization may choose to approach process improvement from the perspective of either process area capability or organizational maturity. Simply put, a process area capability perspective focuses on establishing baselines and measuring improvement results in each area individually. This approach is supported in a continuous representation, with its use of the key term "capability." In contrast, an organizational maturity perspective emphasizes sets of process areas that are intended to define proven stages of process maturity across an organization. This approach is employed in a staged representation, with its use of the key term "maturity."

5.1. Staged Models

A staged model provides a predefined road map for organizational improvement based on proven grouping and ordering of processes and associated organizational relationships. The term "staged" comes from the way that the model describes this road map—namely, as a series of "stages" that are called "maturity levels." Each maturity level has a set of process areas that indicate where an organization should focus to improve its organizational process. In turn, each process area is described in terms of the practices that contribute to satisfying its goals. The practices describe the infrastructure and activities that contribute most to the effective implementation and institutionalization of the process areas. Progress occurs by satisfying the goals of all process areas in a particular maturity level.[4]

---

3. See Section 5.3.3 for a discussion of the use of generic goals.
4. The concept of five stages or maturity levels goes back to Crosby in *Quality Is Free*, which described a five-level scale with "world-class" as level 5. Actually, Crosby's proposed scale is

Appraisals against a staged model evaluate the organization as a whole by determining which of the process areas have been achieved—that is, how many goals have been met. Based on the satisfied process areas, the organization is assigned a single maturity level. When you hear that a corporation "is at maturity level 3," for example, it means that the organization has conducted an appraisal and satisfied all goals associated with the process areas included in maturity levels 2 and 3 of a staged model.

5.2. Continuous Models

Continuous models provide less specific guidance on the order in which improvement should be accomplished. These models are called continuous because they lack discrete stages and, therefore, have no concept of organizational maturity. EIA 731 is an example of a continuous model.

Like staged models, continuous models have process areas that contain practices. Unlike in staged models, however, the practices of a process area in a continuous model are organized in a manner that supports individual process area growth and improvement. Most of the practices associated with process improvement are generic; they are external to the individual process areas and apply to all process areas.[5] The generic practices are grouped into capability levels, each of which has a definition that is roughly equivalent to the definition of the maturity levels in a staged model. Process areas are improved and institutionalized by implementing the generic practices in those process areas. In a continuous model such as EIA 731, goals are not specifically stated, which puts even more emphasis on practices. The collective capability levels of all process areas determine organizational improvement, and an organization can tailor a continuous model so as to target only certain process areas for improvement. In other words, the organization can create its own "staging" of process areas.

---

closer to capability levels in a continuous model than to maturity levels in a staged model, because he applied a similar scale across many areas. Section 5.2 describes the capability levels in a continuous model.

5. EIA 731 introduced the concept of advanced practices. These technical practices within a process area (called a *focus area* in 731) are associated with higher capability levels and so augment the generic practices.

In a continuous appraisal, each process area is rated at its own capability level. An organization will most likely have different process areas rated at different capability levels. The results of this rating can be reported as a capability profile, like that shown in Figure 5-1.

The capability profile may include just the level number ratings, as in Figure 5-2, or it may also contain detailed information at the goal or practice levels. The latter option provides more specific information in graphical form by highlighting the findings (i.e., weaknesses and strengths) with different colors. Typically, profiles are created via a spreadsheet.

Capability profiles can also be used to define a target for process improvement activities in an organization. Because a target profile shows the desired capability profile at a specific point in time, it can be used to show progress along the process improvement journey.

Another way to use capability profiles is to organize the process dimension so that it represents the staged maturity levels. For example, a series of profiles may be used to set goals for the organization or to evaluate the results of an appraisal using equivalent staging (Section 5.3.3 describes the application of this concept to CMMI). In addition, capability profiles can be defined for subsets of process areas when different parts of the organization own the processes related to them. Alternatively, the same process areas may be included in multiple

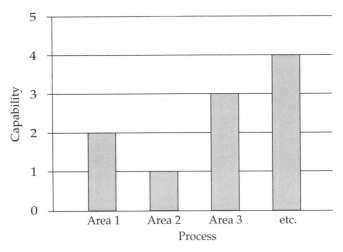

Figure 5-1: *Simple capability level*

owners' target profiles. When the entire organization undergoes an appraisal, the process areas are rated as a whole.

5.3. CMMI Model Representations

The CMMI Team was given an unprecedented challenge: Create a single model that could be viewed from two distinct perspectives, continuous and staged. This mandate meant that each representation should include the same basic information for process improvement. As a consequence, a CMMI process appraisal that addressed the same scope should result in the same findings, no matter which model representation was used during the appraisal.

5.3.1 Selection of Process Areas

As described in Chapter 4, a major challenge centered on the selection of the process areas for CMMI.[6] A second, even thornier issue was whether the process areas in the two representations would need to be (or should be) identical.[7] The team employed a well-defined set of criteria in identifying process areas. That is, a process area was defined as containing a related set of activities that, if performed, would result in a high probability of significant improvement in the area, thereby aiding in the achievement of business objectives for the organization.[8]

For example, the inadequate definition or management of project requirements is frequently mentioned in trying to understand what went wrong in a given program. Furthermore, a set of recognized activities exists that, if performed, would go a long way toward correcting

---

6. As discussed in Chapter 3, the CMMI Team did not start with a blank slate. Its task was not to create a new model from scratch, but rather to integrate (initially) three existing models. Each of these models already had process areas identified, and these areas made up the initial set of candidates. Team members then considered the hopes or expectations among users of the CMMI source models that process areas to which they were accustomed would remain in CMMI.

7. In this section, we invite the reader to enter (briefly) this "briar patch"—not to share the pain (well, maybe a little), but to provide some insight. You can, of course, decline the invitation. The bottom line (which you need to know) is that the two CMMI representations have the same process areas, specific goals, and specific practices.

8. A variety of other criteria for what makes a good process area exist, including the following: A process area tells you what to do, not how to do it or who should do it; it can be implemented in multiple organizational and product contexts; and it has sufficient cohesion and granularity to be separately implemented, rated, and improved.

what might have gone wrong with requirements. As a consequence, it should come as no surprise that CMMI includes two process areas related to this topic: Requirements Development and Requirements Management. No debate occurs regarding whether process areas such as Requirements Development and Requirements Management would be appropriate in both a staged representation and a continuous representation. Whichever architectural representation was to be adopted for the model, both areas would be of critical importance.

But suppose that the CMMI Team had been asked to proceed differently. That is, imagine it had been asked not to develop one model with two representations, but rather a single model representation (e.g., continuous, staged, or some hybrid). It is not clear that the resultant list of process areas would have been exactly identical for each of the various possible single model representations. In other words, the process areas needed in a staged representation and the process areas needed in a continuous representation are not necessarily the same.

For example, in a staged model, the process areas exist at a single maturity level only; they do not span levels. Requirements Management is a process area staged at maturity level 2; no parts of the Requirements Management process area exist at higher maturity levels. Thus, as an organization works to achieve maturity levels 3, 4, or 5, it need not tackle additional tasks that come from the Requirements Management process area.

Of course, the organization should not ignore the maturity level 2 process areas as it moves ahead to higher maturity levels. To be an organization at maturity level 3 means (in general) that the processes used on projects are tailored from the organization's standard set of processes. This approach includes the management of requirements; a standard set of processes should exist for handling requirements management across the organization, and individual projects should derive their specific processes for requirements management from that standard set.

In CMMI, the Integrated Project Management (IPM) process area, which is staged at maturity level 3, expects an organization to return to the process areas from maturity level 2 (such as Requirements Management) and perform them in a manner consistent with maturity level 3 expectations. In IPM, a goal for a project is to use a defined process that is tailored from the organization's set of standard processes.

Moving from the staged representation to the continuous representation, a generic practice at capability level 3 (GP 3.1) also sets the expectation for a defined process. In Requirements Management, for example, GP 3.1 reads as follows: "Establish and maintain the description of a defined requirements management process." By performing that practice, and the comparable generic practice in other process areas staged at maturity level 2, the organization may raise each process area to capability level 3 when viewed from the perspective of the continuous representation. The continuous representation does not require an independent mechanism (such as the first goal in IPM) to raise maturity level 2 process areas to maturity level 3. Also, if you look at IPM from a continuous viewpoint, some practices may look like they really belong (perhaps as "advanced" practices) in the Project Planning or Project Monitoring and Control process areas.[9]

We will not explore in detail all of the architectural nuances that might distinguish the two representations. Rather, we simply note that the CMMI team had a choice: allow the process areas to be different in the two representations, or keep them the same. The former option (different process areas) would have allowed for the construction of "better" or "purer" staged or continuous representations, albeit at the cost of potential confusion to those who might need to deal with two representations having different process areas. The latter option (same process areas) would enhance the sense that the two representations are really just one CMMI model with two views, albeit at the cost of potentially confusing duplication or positioning of material in the model, which would be needed to allow both representations to work. The decision was made to have the same process areas in both representations for CMMI.

5.3.2 Organization of Process Areas

The 22 process areas of CMMI for Development are presented in alphabetical order by acronym in the model. They are identified as being in one of four maturity levels in the staged representation and in one of four process categories in the continuous representation. For example,

---

9. As we noted at the start of this chapter, all advanced practices were removed from the model in CMMI version 1.2. If and when CMMI evolves to a single representation, perhaps the potential role of advanced practices should be reexamined. They represent a powerful mechanism to enrich capability level definitions within individual process areas.

for Decision and Analysis Resolution the following is stated under the process area name: "A Support Process Area at Maturity Level 3."

Tables 5-1 and 5-2 show the staged and continuous groupings of the process areas for CMMI for Development, respectively.

Table 5-1: *Staged Groupings*

Staged Grouping	*Acronyms*	*Process Areas*
Maturity level 2	REQM	Requirements Management
	PP	Project Planning
	PMC	Project Monitoring and Control
	SAM	Supplier Agreement Management
	MA	Measurement and Analysis
	PPQA	Process and Product Quality Assurance
	CM	Configuration Management
Maturity level 3	RD	Requirements Development
	TS	Technical Solution
	PI	Product Integration
	VER	Verification
	VAL	Validation
	OPF	Organizational Process Focus
	OPD+IPPD	Organizational Process Definition+IPPD
	OT	Organizational Training
	IPM+IPPD	Integrated Project Management+IPPD
	RSKM	Risk Management
	DAR	Decision Analysis and Resolution

Staged Grouping	Acronyms	Process Areas
Maturity level 4	OPP	Organizational Process Performance
	QPM	Quantitative Project Management
Maturity level 5	OID	Organizational Innovation and Deployment
	CAR	Causal Analysis and Resolution

Table 5-2: *Continuous Groupings*

Continuous Grouping	Acronyms	Process Areas
Process Management	OPF	Organizational Process Focus
	OPD+IPPD	Organizational Process Definition+IPPD
	OT	Organizational Training
	OPP	Organizational Process Performance
	OID	Organizational Innovation and Deployment
Project Management	PP	Project Planning
	PMC	Project Monitoring and Control
	SAM	Supplier Agreement Management
	IPM+IPPD	Integrated Project+IPPD Management
	RSKM	Risk Management
	QPM	Quantitative Project Management

(*continued*)

Table 5-2: *Continuous Groupings (continued)*

Continuous Grouping	Acronyms	Process Areas
Engineering	REQM	Requirements Management
	RD	Requirements Development
	TS	Technical Solution
	PI	Product Integration
	VER	Verification
	VAL	Validation
Support	CM	Configuration Management
	PPQA	Process and Product Quality Assurance
	MA	Measurement and Analysis
	DAR	Decision Analysis and Resolution
	CAR	Causal Analysis and Resolution

5.3.3 Equivalent Staging

To reinforce the concept of one model with representations, CMMI provides a mapping to move from the continuous perspective to the staged perspective. For maturity levels 2 and 3, this concept is straightforward and easy to understand. If an organization using the continuous representation has achieved capability level 2 in the seven process areas that make up maturity level 2 (in the staged representation), then it can be said to have achieved maturity level 2 (Figure 5-2).

Similarly, if an organization using the continuous representation has achieved capability level 3 in the 7 process areas that make up maturity level 2 and the 11 process areas that make up maturity level 3 (a total of 18 process areas in CMMI for Development), then it can be said to have achieved maturity level 3 (Figure 5-3).

For maturity levels 4 and 5, a similar mechanism is not available to define an equivalent staging. For example, maturity level 4 in the

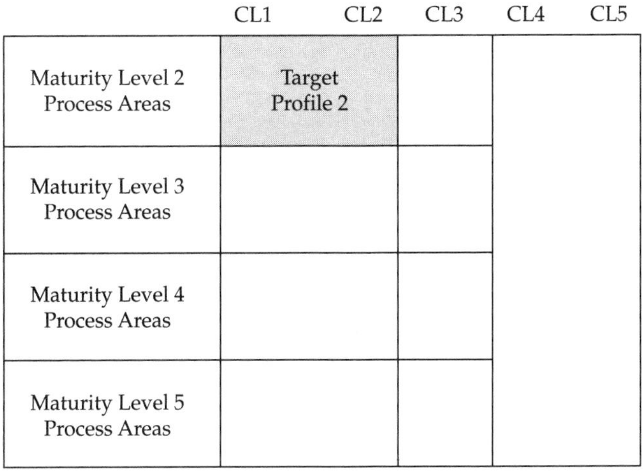

	CL1	CL2	CL3	CL4	CL5
Maturity Level 2 Process Areas	Target Profile 2				
Maturity Level 3 Process Areas					
Maturity Level 4 Process Areas					
Maturity Level 5 Process Areas					

Figure 5-2: *Target profile 2*

staged representation does not require that the kinds of activities found in this level occur in each and every process area. Nor is quantitative management of processes or subprocesses required for any given process area. One organization that achieves maturity level 4 may conduct quantitative management in one set of areas, whereas another organization may handle quantitative management in another set of

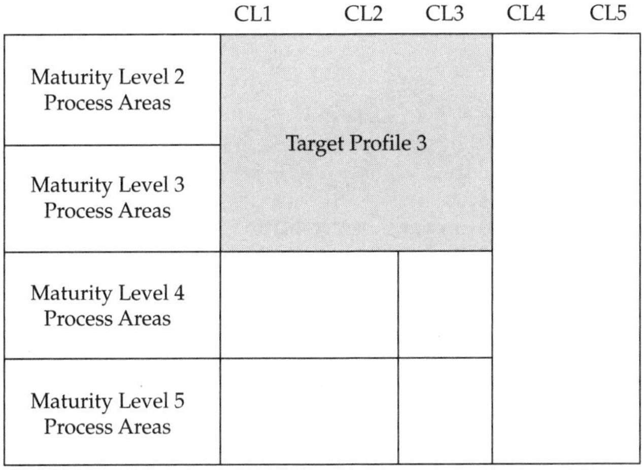

	CL1	CL2	CL3	CL4	CL5
Maturity Level 2 Process Areas	Target Profile 3				
Maturity Level 3 Process Areas					
Maturity Level 4 Process Areas					
Maturity Level 5 Process Areas					

Figure 5-3: *Target profile 3*

areas; there may be no overlap between the two sets, and yet both organizations may operate at maturity level 4. Thus, in Figure 5-4, we cannot highlight any particular process area as being capability level 4 and claim that it is required for an equivalent staging to maturity level 4.

Instead, to obtain an equivalent staging for maturity level 4, we require that an organization meet the goals up through capability level 3 in the process areas that are staged at maturity levels, 2, 3, and 4. This idea may sound confusing, but it is correct. Table 5-3 details the three goals of the two maturity level 4 process areas. To achieve capability level 3 in these two process areas means two things:

1. The three specific goals in Table 5-3 are met: The project is quantitatively managed, subprocesses are statistically managed to meet quality and process performance objectives, and baselines and models for expected process performance exist.

2. A defined process is used for the activities performed to achieve these goals.

These items are exactly what would need to be established for maturity level 4, based on the CMMI staged representation. Consequently, to be rated at maturity level 4, some subprocesses in some process areas must be statistically managed, but it is not possible to specify in advance which process areas are targeted. In a real-life capability profile for an organization at maturity level 4, the capability level of at least one process area would be at level 4.

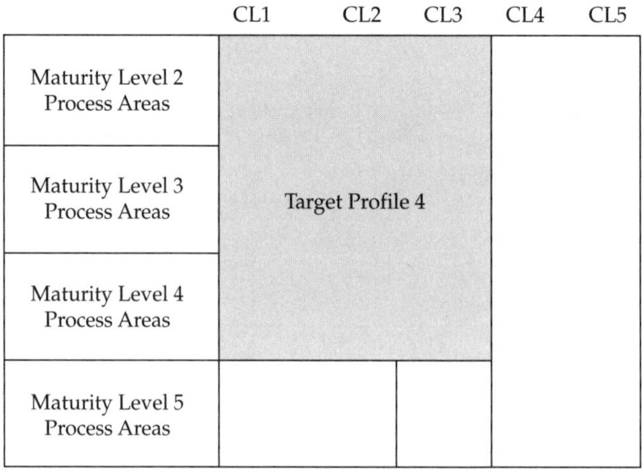

Figure 5-4: *Target profile 4*

Table 5-3: *Maturity Level 4 Process Areas and Goals*

Process Area	Specific Goals
Quantitative Project Management (QPM)	SG 1: The project is quantitatively managed using quality and process-performance objectives. SG 2: The performance of selected subprocesses within the project's defined process is statistically managed.
Organizational Process Performance (OPP)	SG 1: Baselines and models that characterize the expected process performance of the organization's set of standard processes are established and maintained.

The equivalent staging for maturity level 5 is handled in a similar way (Figure 5-5). In this manner, the user of the continuous representation could establish a maturity level rating, if desired, for any maturity level (1 through 5).

For CMMI, if an organization wanted to have a single-number rating of a maturity level, then it could choose a CMMI staged representation.

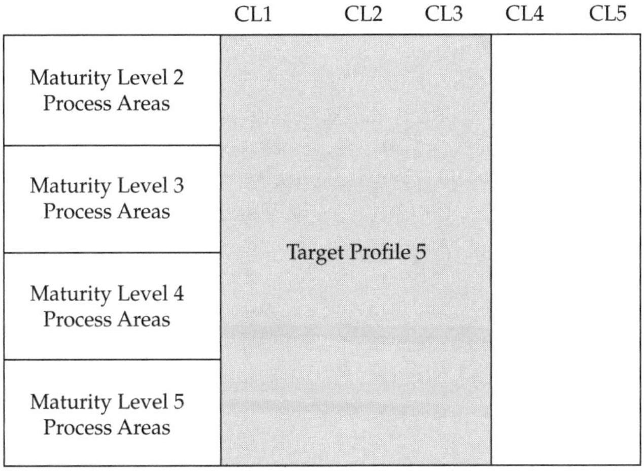

Figure 5-5: *Target profile 5*

Of course, because this equivalent staging comprises a set of four target profiles, the organization could also choose a CMMI continuous representation.

5.4. Conclusion

Two representations of the CMMI model have been developed: continuous and staged. With each new release of the model, the differences between these representations have dwindled to the point that there is currently little to discuss. In the next version of the CMMI Framework, this consideration will likely cease to exist altogether.

For now, however, model users need to select which version (or versions) of the model from the CMMI Product Suite they will use; we will discuss considerations related to that decision in Chapter 8. When the time comes to make a selection, the information in this chapter, which focuses on what distinguishes the two representations, should provide you with the basic understanding that you will need to make an informed choice.

Chapter 6

CMMI Dimensions for Measuring Improvement

Catch, then, oh catch the transient hour;
Improve each moment as it flies!
Samuel Johnson, *Winter: An Ode* (1709–1784)

Anyone who isn't confused really doesn't understand the situation.
Edward R. Murrow (1908–1965)

Chapter 5 presented some basic information about the two CMMI representations, continuous and staged. This chapter continues to explore the relationships between the two representations by taking a more detailed look at how the capability and maturity dimensions are implemented in CMMI.[1] Essentially, the differences in the two representations reflect the methods used to describe the process dimension

---

1. At some point in our description of the two CMMI architectural representations, you may ask, "Which representation should I use?" When that point comes, you may wish to turn to Chapter 8, which covers picking a representation. In Chapter 6, we focus on building a good understanding of these structures and their implementation in CMMI.

for each capability or maturity level. Rest assured that while the mechanics of the descriptions may differ, both representations achieve the same improvement purposes through the use of generic goals and practices as required and expected model elements.

Continuous models describe improvement by focusing on capability within individual process areas. Capability levels for a process area are defined by the generic goals. An organization reaches a particular process area capability level when it has satisfied all of the specific goals, all of the generic goals defined for that level, and all of the generic goals from lower levels. Looking at a number of process area capability levels creates a "continuous" profile of the organization's capability.

Staged models describe the maturity of organizations through success-ful implementation of ordered groups of process areas. These groups, or stages, improve processes together, based on achievements in the previous stage. Each process area in the staged model includes the appropriate generic goals and practices for its stage.

This chapter discusses in detail the characteristics and mechanisms used by CMMI in defining the capability dimension, the maturity dimension, generic practices, and staging. Chapter 7 addresses the process dimensions for both representations.

6.1 Capability Dimension

The capability dimension is used in the continuous representation of CMMI, just as it was in CMMI's predecessor source model, EIA 731 (see Section 3.3.2). To start this chapter, we describe the capability levels in CMMI and summarize the mechanism of capability improvement. Section 6.3 offers a more detailed discussion of the individual generic practices.

CMMI includes six levels of process area capability, imaginatively called *capability levels* (*CLs*), and numbered 0 through 5. These CLs indi-cate how well the organization performs in an individual process area. As shown in Figure 6-1, capability level 0 (CL 0) indicates that the processes are *Not Performed,* which means that one or more of the spe-cific goals of the process area are not satisfied. The capability levels

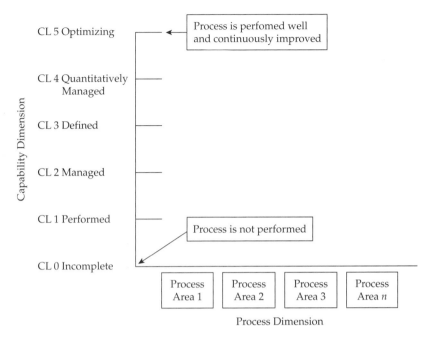

Figure 6-1: *Capability dimension*

increase up to capability level 5 (CL 5), where the process is performed consistently well and is being continuously improved.

Table 6-1 shows the generic goal statements for each capability level. As indicated in the table, no generic goal exists for CL 0 (Not Performed). The reason for not having a goal is that this level simply signifies "not yet CL 1."[2]

Capability level 1 is called *Performed,* and the generic goal for this level focuses on the achievement of the specific goals of the process area. One generic practice is mapped to the CL 1 generic goal; it specifies that the specific practices of the process area are performed at this level of capability. Even though 1 is a lowly number, reaching CL 1 represents a significant achievement for an organization. If a process area is at CL 1, then the specific goals of the process area are satisfied. The added capabilities for CL 2 through CL 5 depend on the specific practices within a

2. It is highly recommended that when describing an organization's capability as "zero" that the words "not yet level 1" be substituted—no one wants to be considered as being at level 0.

Table 6-1: *Generic Goals*

Capability Level	Generic Goal
CL 0	No goal.
CL 1	GG 1: The process supports and enables achievement of the specific goals of the process area by transforming identifiable input work products to produce identifiable output work products.
CL 2	GG 2: The process is institutionalized as a managed process.
CL 3	GG 3: The process is institutionalized as a defined process.
CL 4	GG 4: The process is institutionalized as a quantitatively managed process.
CL 5	GG 5: The process is institutionalized as an optimizing process.

process area being performed at their capability level; only when they are performed can they be improved by satisfying higher-level generic goals. Figure 6-2 illustrates how a process increases in capability.

Capability level 2 is called *Managed,* and its generic goal focuses on institutionalization as a managed process. Ten generic practices are mapped to the CL 2 generic goal. A managed process has increased capability over a performed process; the 10 generic practices provide a definition for that increased capability. In general, a process operating at CL 2 has an organizational policy stating which processes will be used. The projects follow a documented plan and process description. They apply adequate and appropriate resources (including funding, people, and tools), and they maintain appropriate assignment of responsibility and authority. In addition, the projects allow for training of the people performing and supporting the process. Work products are placed under appropriate levels of configuration management. All relevant stakeholders are identified and involved as appropriate. Personnel monitor and control the performance of the process and take corrective action when needed. They objectively evaluate the process,

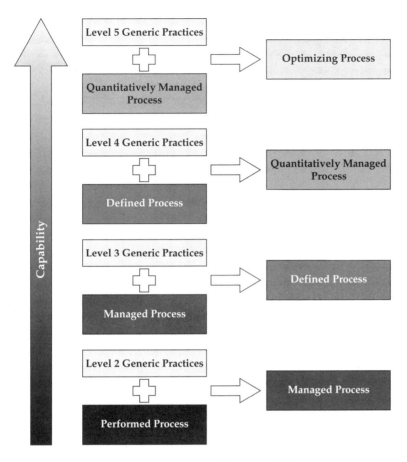

Figure 6-2: *Building capability*

its work products, and its services, and suggest corrective actions where they find noncompliance. The activities, status, and results of the process activities are reviewed with appropriate levels of management, and corrective action is taken if necessary. Thanks to this robust set of generic practices at CL 2, most of which target individual projects, a managed process represents a significant advance relative to a performed process.

Capability level 3 is called *Defined,* and the generic goal for this level focuses on institutionalization as a defined process. In layman's terms, for each process area considered, each project in an organization will have a managed process (like that created under CL 2) that is tailored from the organization's standard processes using standard tailoring guidelines.[3] Two generic practices are mapped to the CL 3 generic goal: Besides the establishment of defined processes, process assets and process measurements must be collected and used for future improvements to the process.

Whereas capability level 2 targets the capability of individual process instances,[4] capability level 3 focuses on organizational standardization and deployment of the processes. Process performance is stabilized across the projects because processes are standardized across the organization; the standard processes, in turn, are tailored for each instance in which that process is needed. Personnel can readily apply their process-based knowledge and skills across multiple instances of the process without expensive retraining.

Capability level 4 is called *Quantitatively Managed,* and its generic goal focuses on institutionalization as a quantitatively managed process. Without getting into the finer points of statistical process control, a CL 4 process is a defined process (like that created under CL 3—see how this inheritance works?) that uses statistical and other quantitative methods to control selected subprocesses. For example, if you know that requirements-related defects for a certain product historically account for less than 5 percent of the total volume and your process measures (as instituted at CL 3) deviate from that percentage significantly, you can be fairly certain that a problem exists and should be investigated.

Because of the overhead involved and to make general common sense, the process measures selected for CL 4 relate to individual subprocesses—not necessarily all processes or even entire processes. Obviously, the organization should quantitatively manage only those subprocesses that are important to its particular business needs and objectives.

Capability level 5 is called *Optimizing,* and the generic goal for this level focuses on institutionalization as an optimizing process. CL 5 is a bit tricky, because it essentially requires the organization to constantly adapt the quantitatively managed subprocesses established at CL 4 based on their measures and established objectives for quality and process performance. This requirement doesn't mean just fixing problems (such as the quality anomaly cited earlier), but also entails analyzing trends, surveying technical practice, addressing common causes of process

---

3. This example assumes the process area considered is a project-related process area—that is, from the Project Management process area category.
4. Usually, each instance of the process is associated with a project.

variation, and then determining how best to adapt the process to changing business needs. This procedure could result in either evolutionary or revolutionary action.

6.2 Maturity Dimension

The maturity dimension of a CMMI model is described in the staged representation. Five levels of maturity exist, each of which indicates the process maturity of the organization. Figure 6-3 shows the *maturity levels (MLs)* and their characteristics.

Note the overlap in the names for maturity levels 2 through 5 and the names for capability levels 2 through 5. Although these capability levels and maturity levels have the same names, they are fundamentally different. A capability level is independently applied to an individual process area, whereas a maturity level specifies a set of process areas whose combined set of goals must be achieved. Furthermore, generic goals and practices follow different inclusion rules in the staged representation than they do in the continuous representation. They are included in the process areas according to the level where the process area is staged. During an appraisal for maturity level 2, for example, the process areas staged at maturity level 2 use the CL 2 generic goal and its associated generic practices. Process areas staged at maturity

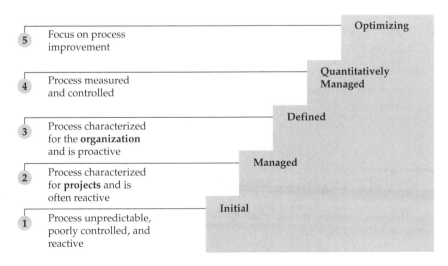

Figure 6-3: *Staged maturity levels*

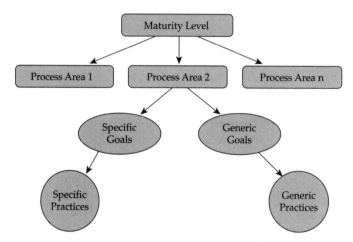

Figure 6-4: *Maturity level structure*

levels 3 through 5 include the CL 3 generic goal, plus the generic practices from both capability levels 2 and 3. The generic goals and practices for capability levels 1, 4, and 5 are not used in the maturity level definitions—no process areas are staged at level 1, and the generic goals for capability levels 4 and 5 are addressed by the specific goals and practices of the four process areas staged at maturity levels 4 and 5.

Note that maturity level 1 has a different name (Initial) from that assigned to capability level 1 (Performed). In the staged representation, ML 1 is similar to CL 0 in its negative connotation; that is, an organization at ML 1 is one that has not yet reached ML 2. No goals need to be met to qualify for ML 1. Unlike CL 1, ML 1 does not connote any significant achievement for an organization.

Figure 6-4 shows the structure of a maturity level. In the staged representation, each process area exists at a maturity level. The process areas required for each staged level were shown in Chapter 5. In Chapter 7, we will describe each of the process areas in detail.

6.3 Generic Practices in the Capability Dimension

In Sections 6.1 and 6.2, we saw how generic goals and practices are used to define both capability levels and maturity levels. The continuous representation includes 17 generic practices grouped by capability levels 1 through 5. As stated earlier, only the capability level 2 and 3 generic practices are included in the staged representation. This section takes a more detailed look at the full set of generic practices used in the continuous representation. Section 6.4 scrutinizes the partial set of generic practices used in the staged representation.

6.3.1 Capability Level 0 Generic Practices

Capability level 0 does not have any generic practices. It is the *Not Performed* level, which means that one or more of the specific goals for a process area are not satisfied.

6.3.2 Capability Level 1 Generic Practices

Table 6-2 shows the single generic practice for capability level 1. When GP 1.1 is applied to a process area, the specific practices of the process area are performed. Although version 1.1 of the CMMI model included both base and advanced specific practices, version 1.2 does not include advanced specific practices.

6.3.3 Capability Level 2 Generic Practices

Table 6-3 shows the generic practices for capability level 2.

GP 2.1 establishes an organizational policy that requires planning and execution of the process area. Organizational policies need not be labeled with the term "policy," but senior management sponsorship must be documented in a manner that requires planning and the use of the processes associated with the process area.

Implementing GP 2.2 establishes the requirements and objectives for the processes associated with the process area, and it forms the basis for

Table 6-2: *Generic Practice from Capability Level 1*

Name	Generic Practice
GP 1.1 Base Practices	Perform the specific practices of the process to develop work products and provide services to achieve the specific goals of the process area.

Table 6-3: *Generic Practices from Capability Level 2*

Name	*Generic Practice*
GP 2.1 Establish an Organizational Policy	Establish and maintain an organizational policy for planning and performing the process.
GP 2.2 Plan the Process	Establish and maintain the plan for performing the process.
GP 2.3 Provide Resources	Provide adequate resources for performing the process, developing the work products, and providing the services of the process.
GP 2.4 Assign Responsibility	Assign responsibility and authority for performing the process, developing the work products, and providing the services of the process.
GP 2.5 Train People	Train the people performing or supporting the process as needed.
GP 2.6 Manage Configurations	Place designated work products of the process under appropriate levels of configuration control.
GP 2.7 Identify and Involve Relevant Stakeholders	Identify and involve the relevant stakeholders as planned.
GP 2.8 Monitor and Control the Process	Monitor and control the process against the plan for performing the process and take appropriate corrective action.
GP 2.9 Objectively Evaluate Adherence	Objectively evaluate adherence of the process against its process description, standards, and procedures, and address noncompliance.
GP 2.10 Review Status with Higher-Level Management	Review the activities, status, and results of the process with higher-level management and resolve issues.

process planning. This GP has five subpractices that provide information on how this feat could be accomplished, dealing with management sponsorship, documenting the process, planning for performing the process, reviewing the process with relevant stakeholders, and revising the process as necessary.

This "Plan the Process" generic practice can create confusion when it is applied to the Project Planning process area, as it seems to entail a need to "plan the plan." This result is actually the desired one; the planning of the activities for the Project Planning process area is a logical and necessary set of tasks in any project. The process for planning a project is one that, like any other process, should be planned.[5]

Another potential source of confusion is the fact that some process areas include a goal or specific practices to establish a strategy or a particular plan. This concept differs from the GP 2.2, in that a specific practice for planning will address detailed product or product component strategies and plans—not planning across the full scope of process area activities. For example, in the Risk Management process area, SP 1.3 establishes and maintains the strategy to be used for risk management and SP 3.1 develops risk mitigation plans for the most important risks to the project. In contrast, the generic practice expects that both of these activities will be planned, along with the other risk management practices.

GP 2.3 is a favorite of all project and program managers. When applied to a process area, it ensures that adequate resources are allocated for carrying out the processes associated with the process area. This practice includes the resources required to develop the work products of the process area and provide the services associated with the process, as well as the need for funding, facilities, people, and tools.

When a project applies GP 2.4 to a process area, responsibility and authority are assigned to perform the processes associated with that area. The three subpractices cover assigning responsibility for personnel who are in charge of the process as well as workers who perform the tasks of the process, and confirming that those individuals understand their responsibilities.

---

5. Only one level of "recursion" exists. Nothing in the model requires you to "plan to plan the plan."

The focus of GP 2.5 is ensuring that process participants are adequately trained. This generic practice includes training of the people who will perform and support the process so that they understand the process sufficiently to perform or support it. The Organizational Training process area provides guidance on how to develop an organizational training program that supports GP 2.5. The generic practice and the process area differ, however, in that the process area provides training practices at the organizational level whereas the generic practice addresses training for each process. Of course, a project may choose to rely on organizational training assets to the extent that they are available.

When a project applies GP 2.6 to a process area, it ensures that the appropriate level of configuration management is maintained for the process work products. Formal configuration management may or may not be expected, and a work product may be subject to different levels of configuration management at different points in time. The Configuration Management process area provides the specific practices needed to manage the selected work products for each project-related process area.

GP 2.7 includes the expectation that all of the affected entities will be involved in the process. The relevant stakeholders are specifically identified and drawn into the process associated with the process area.[6] The three subpractices identify stakeholders, let project planners know who these stakeholders are, and get the stakeholders involved.

GP 2.8 ensures that the process activities are monitored relative to the plan (which was defined in GP 2.2) for executing the process and that corrective actions are taken when necessary. Its seven subpractices provide more detailed information on how to monitor and control processes. The Project Monitoring and Control process area supports this generic practice by providing specific goals and practices for monitoring and taking corrective actions.

Objective evaluation of process and work product performance is provided to a process area through GP 2.9. While a quality assurance group or department may be used to perform the evaluations, the CMMI does not assume any particular organizational structure. Note,

---

6. A relevant stakeholder is a person or role that is affected by or held accountable for a process outcome, and whose involvement in a particular activity is planned.

however, that people who are not directly responsible for managing or performing the process should perform the evaluation to enhance objectivity. The Process and Product Quality Assurance process area supports this generic practice by providing guidance on how to accomplish objective evaluations.

When a project applies GP 2.10 to a process area, its higher-level management will review the activities, status, and results of the process and resolve any outstanding issues with the process performance. Each level of management may have its own needs for information about the process performance. The reviews should be both periodic and event driven.

6.3.4 Capability Level 3 Generic Practices

Table 6-4 shows the generic practices for capability level 3.

GP 3.1 supports the institutionalization of processes by expecting that projects will establish and maintain a defined process tailored from the organization's standard processes. Defined processes may be established for a project or an organizational group; although various parts of the organization may have different defined processes, all will be based on the standard processes. This tailoring provides flexibility to companies that have similar units that are organized differently, while ensuring that the standard processes remain truly standard across the enterprise.

Table 6-4: *Generic Practices from Capability Level 3*

Name	Generic Practice
GP 3.1 Establish a Defined Process	Establish and maintain the description of a defined process.
GP 3.2 Collect Improvement Information	Collect work products, measures, measurement results, and improvement information derived from planning and performing the process to support the future use and improvement of the organization's processes and process assets.

GP 3.1 has five subpractices that support the establishment of the defined process associated with the process area. The Organizational Process Definition process area supports GP 3.1 by providing specific goals and practices related to the establishment of standard processes. The Integrated Project Management process area is also closely related to this generic practice. The notes in the model on individual specific practices offer more information on the use of these processes in an organization.

GP 3.2 serves as a key to further process improvement, because it expects the organization to collect example work products, measures, and other data about the process for future use. Without such historical data, the process may be difficult to plan and impossible to manage quantitatively—the focus of CL 4. Three of the subpractices within GP 3.2 provide information on the contents of the process library; the fourth subpractice captures proposed improvements to the process assets. The Organizational Process Focus process area supports this generic practice by addressing process asset deployment and incorporating process-related experiences into the organizational process assets.

6.3.5 Capability Level 4 Generic Practices

Table 6-5 shows the generic practices for capability level 4.

Table 6-5: *Generic Practices from Capability Level 4*

Name	*Generic Practice*
GP 4.1 Establish Quality Objectives	Establish and maintain quantitative objectives for the process that address quality and process performance based on customer needs and business objectives.
GP 4.2 Stabilize Subprocess Performance	Stabilize the performance of one or more subprocesses to determine the ability of the process to achieve the established quantitative quality and process-performance objectives.

GP 4.1 expects an organization to use its business objectives to define process performance and quality objectives. All relevant stakeholders should participate in this activity. Once established, the quantitative objectives are allocated to the processes. These processes may be related to process areas or to a set of process areas. The Quantitative Project Management (QPM) process area encompasses quantitatively managing processes, so the information in that area is extremely useful in implementing GP 4.1, especially in project-related process areas.

In implementing GP 4.2, the organization uses the quality and process performance objectives to statistically manage selected subprocesses. A strong rationale for choosing the particular subprocesses should exist, and the organization needs to demonstrate how those subprocesses are managed to meet the intent of the generic practice. The Quantitative Project Management process area also supports this generic practice.

6.3.6 Capability Level 5 Generic Practices

Table 6-6 shows the generic practices for capability level 5.

Implementing GP 5.1 drives the organization to select and deploy process and technology improvements that contribute to its ability to meet quality and performance objectives for the process. The Organizational Innovation and Deployment process area provides more information in terms of goals and practices regarding ways to implement this generic practice.

Table 6-6: *Generic Practices from Capability Level 5*

Name	*Generic Practice*
GP 5.1 Ensure Continuous Process Improvement	Ensure continuous improvement of the process in fulfilling the relevant business objectives of the organization.
GP 5.2 Correct Common Cause of Problems	Identify and correct the root causes of defects and other problems in the process.

The root causes of defects in the process are identified and corrected through application of GP 5.2.[7] Without this practice, organizations would find it difficult to gain the agility needed to rapidly solve problems and effectively evolve their processes. Goals and practices that can be applied in implementing GP 5.2 appear in the Causal Analysis and Resolution process area.

6.4 Generic Practices in the Maturity Dimension

The maturity dimension is used in the staged representation for the CMMI model. As discussed in Section 6.2, only the generic goals and practices from capability levels 2 and 3 are used in establishing the maturity dimension. Within this dimension, the generic practices have the exact same meaning that they have in the capability dimension.

6.5 Organizational Capability Evolution

Users of staged models often have difficulty in understanding how a continuous model measures organizational progress. When one is accustomed to a model in which process areas build on one another, it is not always obvious how possibly unrelated process areas might be improved without some kind of staging. Users may also wonder when work should be carried out in a particular process area. Although staged models do not explicitly prohibit addressing higher-level key process areas before lower-level ones, they imply that this sequence should not be the normal way of proceeding. In continuous models, of course, this implication would be meaningless.

The following example may help explain how an ML 4 process area fits into the capability level used in the CMMI model. Quantitative Project Management is an ML 4 process area. Obviously, it doesn't make sense

---

7. The concept of a *root cause* is frequently misunderstood. Clearly, it is not a cause for which no preceding cause exists; only a god or the "big bang" would be a candidate to meet that definition. Rather, a root cause is an antecedent cause of a problem or defect such that, if it were removed, the problem or defect would be lessened or eliminated. Do not confuse a possible solution that may address a root cause with the root cause itself. In other words, avoid characterizing a root cause with a negative formulation such as "Solution A to the problem was not implemented" or "There was a lack of A." Think of a cause as something that was present, not something that was absent.

for an organization to start its process improvement journey with this particular process area. In fact, cautionary statements in the Introductory Notes section of the process area specifically warn against taking this approach. The continuous representation, however, does not dictate the time or the state that must be reached before delving into this—or any other—process area.

When an organization initially establishes a QPM process, it may be rated at CL 1. By adding generic goals and practices, it may improve its capability to CL 5 if deemed appropriate by the organization. In contrast, strict adherence to the staging in the staged representation would not implement QPM until ML 3 has been implemented.[8] The bottom line is that the two means of achieving the advanced capability are striving for the same objective: quantitatively managed processes.

---

8. In EIA 731, the practices in QPM are addressed as advanced practices in other focus areas.

Chapter 7

CMMI Process Areas

Never tell people how to do things. Tell them what to do and they will surprise you with their ingenuity.
General George S. Patton (1885–1945)

In theory, there is no difference between theory and practice. In practice there is.
Yogi Berra (1925–)

All CMMI models are based on 16 process areas called the CMMI Model Foundation (CMF), which defines the process dimension of the model.[1] For a given constellation the CMF core is augmented with non-CMF process areas, which may be required or considered optional based on the constellation needs. Optional process areas are referred to as "additions."[2] Occasionally, a constellation will add specific practices to the CMF, which again may be required or considered optional.

---

1. During the development of the CMMI-ACQ model, some minor changes were made to the CMF materials. A revision of the CMMI-DEV may be released to make the CMF material in both models identical. After all, that is the definition of CMF.
2. You may find that the term "addition" is used with two different meanings: (1) anything added to the CMF core for a given constellation or (2), in a more restrictive sense, those model components whose use for a given constellation is optional. A non-CMF process area that is required for a constellation would be an addition in the first sense, but not in the second. We use the term with the second meaning.

The CMMI for Development model includes six required Development process areas, plus the IPPD addition that adds material to two of the CMF process areas. The CMMI for Acquisition model includes six required Acquisition process areas, plus specific practices added in four CMF process areas. The latest draft of the CMMI for Services model contains an extended version of Requirements Management specifically for Services, five required Services process areas, and three Services process areas that are optional additions.[3]

This chapter provides a brief description of each process area, focusing on its purpose, goals, and specific practices. It also points out some of the inherent relationships between the process areas, which are important in planning process improvement activities.

Process areas are classified by maturity level and by category, where the categories (including all three constellations) are Process Management, Project Management, Support, Engineering, Acquisition, and Service Establishment and Delivery. Table 7-1 shows the process areas grouped by category and their associated maturity level, with CMF or the constellation with which they are associated indicated. If more than

Table 7-1: *Process Areas by Category*

Category	Process Area	Maturity Level	CMF or Constellation
Process Management	Organizational Process Definition +IPPD	3	CMF
	Organizational Process Focus	3	CMF
	Organizational Training	3	CMF
	Organizational Service Management	3	SVC
	Organizational Process Performance	4	CMF

---

3. At the time of this edition of *CMMI Distilled*, the Services constellation was in draft form. The information that follows reflects the current state of this material, but it might (more than likely will) change prior to its release. It is unclear whether the services information will be labeled with the term "constellation" or some other term, but it will be included in some form in the CMMI Product Suite. The CMMI framework architecture may change to better accommodate new areas of interest.

Category	Process Area	Maturity Level	CMF or Constellation
Project Management	Organizational Innovation and Deployment	5	CMF
	Project Monitoring and Control	2	CMF
	Project Planning	2	CMF
	Supplier Agreement Management	2	DEV, SVC
	Capability and Availability Management	3	SVC
	Integrated Project Management +IPPD	3	CMF
	Risk Management	3	CMF
	Service Continuity	3	SVC
	Quantitative Project Management	4	CMF
Support	Configuration Management	2	CMF
	Measurement and Analysis	2	CMF
	Process and Product Quality Assurance	2	CMF
	Decision Analysis and Resolution	3	CMF
	Problem Management	3	SVC
	Causal Analysis and Resolution	5	CMF
Engineering	Requirements Management	2	CMF
	Requirements Management +SVC	2	SVC
	Product Integration	3	DEV
	Requirements Development	3	DEV
	Technical Solution	3	DEV

(continued)

Table 7-1: *Process Areas by Category (continued)*

Category	Process Area	Maturity Level	CMF or Constellation
	Validation	3	DEV
	Verification	3	DEV
Acquisition	Acquisition Requirements Development	2	ACQ
	Agreement Management	2	ACQ
	Solicitation and Supplier Agreement Management	2	ACQ
	Acquisition Technical Management	3	ACQ
	Acquisition Validation	3	ACQ
	Acquisition Verification	3	ACQ
Service Establishment and Delivery	Incident and Request Management	3	SVC
	Service Delivery	3	SVC
	Service System Development	3	SVC
	Service Transition	3	SVC

one constellation is listed, then that process area is part of each of the constellations listed.

We'll review the process areas in the CMMI foundation first (Section 7.1), followed by the two released constellations (CMMI-DEV in Section 7.2 and CMMI-ACQ in Section 7.3). Next we review the draft material from CMMI-SVC (Section 7.4), and finally we conclude the chapter with observations regarding the relationships within CMMI components (Section 7.5). Throughout this chapter we present the process areas by category; this allows us to clarify the process area relationships that emerge when planning a successful process improvement strategy.

7.1 Foundation Process Areas

7.1.1 Foundation Process Management Process Areas

Five process areas make up the Process Management category in the CMF:

- Organizational Process Definition +IPPD (OPD+IPPD)
- Organizational Process Focus (OPF)
- Organizational Process Performance (OPP)
- Organizational Innovation and Deployment (OID)
- Organizational Training (OT)

These process areas address an organization's efforts to define, plan, deploy, implement, monitor, control, verify, measure, and improve its processes. As shown in Figure 7-1, a close relationship exists between four of these process areas. OPP builds on the capabilities in OPF and OPD; OID builds on the capabilities of the other Process Management process areas. This relationship is defined in the staged representation, with OPF and OPD being at ML 3, OPP being at ML 4, and OID being at ML 5. When using the CMMI continuous representation for process improvement, you should consider these relationships and plan your improvement projects accordingly. For example, it is not wise to seek a

© 2008 by Carnegie Mellon University.

Figure 7-1: *Process Management process area relationships*

capability level in OPP that is greater than what you have achieved in both OPF and OPD.

7.1.1.1 Organizational Process Definition

The purpose of Organizational Process Definition is to establish and maintain a usable set of organizational process assets and work environment standards.[4] OPD also has an addition that addresses IPPD. OPD (see Figure 7-2) has one specific goal in the foundation: to create and maintain organizational process assets.[5] OPD and OPF work together, in that the former provides guidance for an organization on creating processes and their supporting assets, while the latter provides guidance on identifying and planning process improvements.

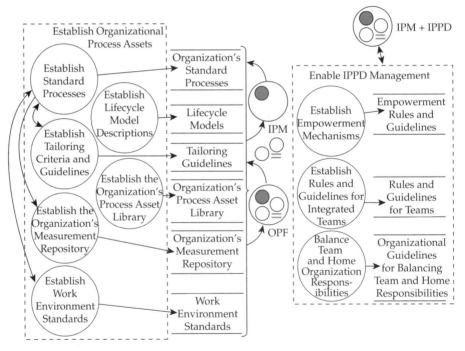

Figure 7-2: *Organizational Process Definition context diagram*

---

4. For the italicized purpose statement that begins each process area, we lift exact wording from the model, with some compression when this statement is rather lengthy.

5. We will begin our description of each (CMMI-DEV and CMMI-ACQ) process area with a context diagram and the purpose statement from the model. The context diagrams are drawn from CMMI training materials: Introduction to CMMI, Version 1.2, and CMMI for Acquisition Supplement for Introduction to CMMI, Version 1.2.

The OPD goal—creating and maintaining organizational process assets—is approached through six specific practices. The first establishes the organization's set of standard processes; typically, this set includes technical, management, administrative, support, and organizational processes. The second practice establishes descriptions of life-cycle models that may be used by each project. The third practice provides tailoring guidelines and criteria for the standard processes, which are in turn used by the projects during the planning phases of the project life cycle.

The fourth specific practice provides a repository for organizational process measurements. An organizational measurement repository supports process performance and quantitative process management as the organization's capability and maturity improve. It also supports the use of historical data in establishing estimates.

The fifth specific practice establishes a library of process assets that are used by the projects. The process asset library supports projects in planning their project-unique processes through tailoring and implementation of the standard processes, with resultant cost savings. This library may contain document templates, example plans, work products, policies, and other process enablers.

The sixth specific practice provides work environment standards for the organization and projects. Work environment standards support the use of common tools, training, and maintenance when they are employed by the projects on a consistent basis.

The IPPD addition includes one specific goal and three specific practices. The goal provides rules and guidelines that govern the operation of integrated teams; the specific practices are used to satisfy this goal. The first of these specific practices establishes empowerment mechanisms to allow teams to make timely decisions. The second defines rules and guidelines for structuring and forming integrated teams. The third specific practice establishes guidelines to help teams balance their team and organizational responsibilities.

Note that the context diagram in Figure 7-2 (and the other context diagrams in this chapter) shows how typical work products of the practices may be used. Because our objective in this book is to introduce each process area, we won't discuss every specific practice or every arrow to or from a typical work product in the context diagram. For further information, refer to the model itself or take a formal CMMI training course. Our objective here is simply to introduce each process area.

7.1.1.2 Organizational Process Focus

The purpose of Organizational Process Focus is to plan, implement, and deploy organizational process improvements based on a thorough understanding of the current strengths and weaknesses of the organization's processes and process assets. OPF uses three specific goals to achieve this purpose: one for determining improvement opportunities, one for planning and implementing selected improvements, and one for deploying the process assets and incorporating lessons learned. The specific practices mapped to each of these goals are shown in the context diagram in Figure 7-3.

For the first goal (determining process improvement opportunities), the organization establishes and maintains its process needs and objectives. These considerations are based on information that is gathered as part of continuous business outcomes monitoring and process review

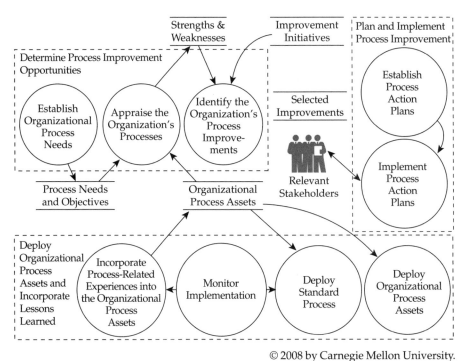

© 2008 by Carnegie Mellon University.

Figure 7-3: *Organizational Process Focus context diagram*

(e.g., measurement, peer reviews, testing, process and product quality assurance, customer feedback, iteration retrospectives), through periodic appraisal activities (such as CMMI or ISO), and from special case reviews associated with causal analysis or improvement initiatives. The organization periodically reviews its objectives to select and prioritize which improvements to make.

The second goal (planning and implementing selected process improvement activities) is carried out with two specific practices. The organization establishes and then implements process action plans to carry out the selected improvements.

In the third goal (deploying the process assets and incorporating lessons learned), the organization's set of standard processes and other process assets with changes to them are deployed to existing and new projects, and the assets are incorporated into the process asset library. The use of the standard process assets is monitored on all projects, measurements related to the use of process assets are analyzed, and lessons learned are identified.

7.1.1.3 Organizational Process Performance

The purpose of Organizational Process Performance is to establish and maintain a quantitative understanding of the performance of the organization's set of standard processes, and to provide the process performance data, baselines, and models to quantitatively manage the organization's projects. OPP (see Figure 7-4) has one specific goal to establish these performance baselines and models. This "advanced" process area builds on both OPD and OPF by establishing expectations and objectives for the quantitative management of quality and process performance. Selected processes or subprocesses are analyzed, perhaps by examining both performance measures and product measures (e.g., quality).[6] Process-performance objectives, baselines, and models are then established. The baselines measure the performance of the organization's standard processes at

---

6. In CMMI, the term "subprocess" connotes a process that is part of a larger process, with the subprocess itself possibly being decomposed into smaller subprocesses, until finally you reach "process elements," which typically are activities or tasks. You will see the term "subprocess" used a lot in the process areas that are staged at maturity levels 4 and 5. This usage occurs because quantitative management, which is the cornerstone of the higher maturity levels, usually occurs with a focus on restricted pieces of a process. For example, an organization may quantitatively manage defects or errors found during reviews, which are a subprocess within the verification process.

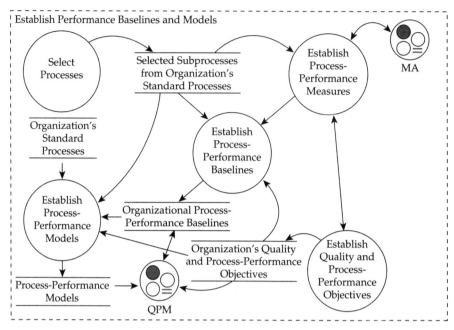

Figure 7-4: *Organizational Process Performance context diagram*

various levels of detail. Of course, tailoring and other factors (such as product line, complexity, application domain, or team size and experience) can significantly affect the baselines. As a result, the organization may need to establish several different performance baselines.

The specific practices in OPP are stated at a high level, and particular attention must be given to the informative materials to fully understand the intent of the process area. [7]

7.1.1.4 Organizational Innovation and Deployment

The purpose of Organizational Innovation and Deployment is to select and deploy incremental and innovative improvements that measurably improve the organization's processes and technologies. The improvements support the organization's quality and process performance objectives, as derived from the organization's business objectives. OID (see Figure 7-5) adds further capability

---

7. At recent conferences that highlight CMMI issues, there have been many presentations on ways to understand performance baselines and models. For example, look at the NDIA Web site (www.ndia.org) for the conference proceedings from the CMMI conference that is held each year in November.

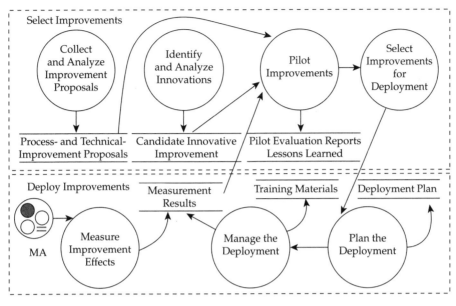

© 2008 by Carnegie Mellon University.

Figure 7-5: *Organizational Innovation and Deployment context diagram*

to OPD, OPF, and OPP with its two goals: selecting process and technology improvements and systematically deploying those improvements.

The CMMI models include technology in the OID process area. Technology is also addressed, at least at the subprocess level and dealing with product technology, in the Technical Solution (TS) process area. In OID, both product- and process-related technologies are deployed to improve the organization.

The first OID goal—selecting improvements—involves collecting and analyzing process and technology improvement proposals. These proposals may come from a variety of places; strategic and operating plans, program risk analyses, capability evaluation results, product defects and errors, industry trends, and customer and user needs and problems are all possibilities. The initiatives proposed may be either incremental or innovative in nature, and the second OID specific practice highlights innovative change.[8] Once opportunities for change have

---

8. In CMMI, the term "innovation" implies something that goes beyond a standard "incremental" improvement—something that may come from outside of the organization—and that represents a major (perhaps revolutionary) change in the way in which business is conducted.

been identified, they are evaluated through pilot projects (as needed) and then selected for deployment. When selecting opportunities to pursue, factors to consider include needed resources, anticipated benefits, risk analysis, schedule, effects on stakeholders, the approach and tools to be used, and the business case for the change.

The second OID goal—deploying improvements—includes planning and managing the deployment of changes, and then measuring the effectiveness of the new process or technology as well as its effects on other management objectives.[9]

This process area reminds us that an improvement initiative is like a project and should be managed as such. As we noted with OPP, the practices in OID are stated at a high level, and particular attention must be given to the informative materials to fully understand the intent of the process area.

7.1.1.5 Organizational Training

The purpose of Organizational Training is to develop the skills and knowledge of people so they can perform their roles effectively and efficiently. OT (see Figure 7-6) has two specific goals: one for establishing an organizational training capability and another for providing the necessary training. This process area does not build on the capability level of any other Process Management process area. Rather, OT supports the organization's strategic and cross-project training needs and ensures that practitioners understand and can correctly use process assets, including organizational standard processes.

The first goal (establishing an organizational training capability) includes four specific practices. First, strategic training needs are established to guide the overall organizational training. Second, responsibility for each need is assigned to either the organization or the project. Third, a tactical plan is established to ensure that training needs are met. This plan should address training topics, schedules, methods, standards for training materials, resources, roles and responsibilities; in short, it should explain how each of the organization's training needs will be addressed. The fourth practice addresses the actual establishment of the organization's training capability, such as developing or

---

9. It can be a difficult challenge to measure the effects of making one change in an environment where many other things also may be changing. Nonetheless, CMMI expects an effort along these lines.

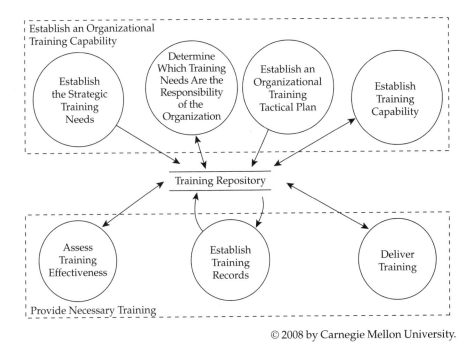

Figure 7-6: *Organizational Training context diagram*

obtaining training materials, identifying instructors, and producing a description of the training curriculum.

Under the second goal (providing necessary training), the specific practices focus on delivery (following the tactical plan) of training to the target audiences, maintenance of training records, and assessment of the effectiveness of the organization's training program.

7.1.2 Foundation Project Management Process Areas

The Project Management foundation process areas cover the activities related to planning, monitoring, and controlling a project. The model foundation includes five Project Management process areas:

- Project Planning (PP)
- Project Monitoring and Control (PMC)
- Integrated Project Management +IPPD (IPM+IPPD)
- Quantitative Project Management (QPM)
- Risk Management (RSKM)

The Integrated Project Management process area is expanded when IPPD is used.

This section describes the Project Management process areas in the CMMI for Development constellation. As shown in Figure 7-7, a close relationship exists between four of these process areas, with IPM and QPM building on the capabilities of PP and PMC. This relationship is defined in the staged representation, with PP and PMC being at ML 2, IPM being at ML 3, and QPM being at ML 4. When using the continuous representation for process improvement, you should understand this relationship and plan your improvement projects accordingly.

7.1.2.1 Project Planning

The purpose of Project Planning is to establish and maintain plans that define project activities. PP (see Figure 7-8) has three specific goals: to establish estimates, to develop a project plan, and to obtain commitments to the plan. PP and PMC work together, in that the former involves the creation of the project plans, and the latter involves tracking progress against the plans. It is through PMC that corrective actions are managed to closure.

In the first goal, which consists of establishing estimates of project planning parameters for the project, the scope of the project is estimated

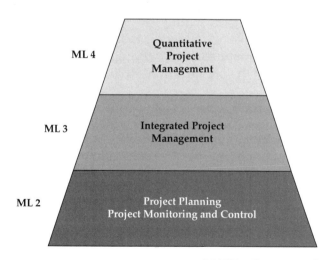

© 2008 by Carnegie Mellon University.

Figure 7-7: *Project Management process area relationships*

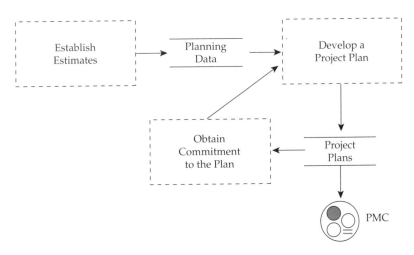

Figure 7-8: *Project Planning context diagram*

based on a work breakdown structure, and project attributes for work products and tasks are estimated. To set the scope of the planning effort, a project life cycle is defined. Estimates of effort and cost for work products and tasks can then be developed. Subsequently, these estimates are used as the basis for developing the project plans in the second goal—budgets and schedules are established, risks are identified, and plans are created for data management, resources, knowledge and skills needed, and stakeholder involvement.

Obtaining commitments to the plan involves making sure that you understand all the project commitments, reconciling the project plan to reflect available and projected resources, and obtaining commitments from relevant stakeholders responsible for performing and supporting plan execution.

7.1.2.2 Project Monitoring and Control

The purpose of Project Monitoring and Control is to provide an understanding of the project's progress so that appropriate corrective actions can be taken when the project's performance deviates significantly from the plan. PMC (see Figure 7-9) has two specific goals: one on monitoring actual performance against the plan, and another on managing corrective actions.

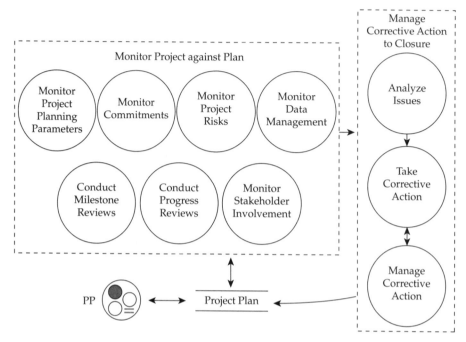

© 2008 by Carnegie Mellon University.

Figure 7-9: *Project Monitoring and Control context diagram*

The first goal—monitor the project against the plan—has five practices that identify what should be monitored and two practices that deal with reviews. The monitoring focuses on the following:

- Project planning parameters
- Commitments
- Project risks
- Data management
- Stakeholder involvement

These monitoring efforts are reviewed at both progress reviews and milestone reviews.

Whenever these monitoring activities and reviews find anomalies and needed corrective actions, the second goal provides specific practices to analyze the issues, initiate the necessary corrective action, and manage the corrective action to closure. Note that other CMMI process areas (such as Verification, Supplier Agreement Management, and Configuration Management) refer to this PMC goal and its practices to provide information about managing corrective actions.

7.1.2.3 Integrated Project Management

The purpose of Integrated Project Management is to establish and manage the project and the involvement of the relevant stakeholders according to an integrated and defined process that is tailored from the organization's set of standard processes. IPM (see Figure 7-10) has two specific goals in the CMMI for Development constellation; adding IPPD provides another specific goal. The two basic goals relate to actually using the project's defined process and to coordinating activities with relevant stakeholders. These goals build on the planning covered in PP, by ensuring that the appropriate organizations and people are involved in managing the project. The organization's set of standard processes, which was developed in the OPD process area, is the basis for the project's defined process.

The first IPM goal has six practices that address how the project follows a defined process tailored from the set of standard processes.

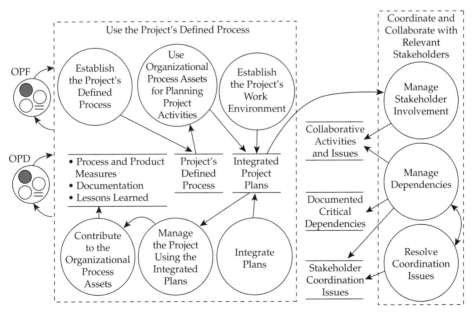

© 2008 by Carnegie Mellon University.

Figure 7-10: *Integrated Project Management (without IPPD) context diagram*

Establishing and maintaining the project's defined process is the first step, with the organization's standard processes serving as a starting point. Next, the organizational process assets from the organizational process asset library are used for planning project activities, establishing the project's work environment, integrating all plans to describe the defined process, and managing the project using the integrated plans. Finally, the project contributes its work products as appropriate (including measures and lessons learned) to the organization's process assets for use by future projects and for process improvement activities.

The second basic goal—coordination and collaboration with relevant stakeholders—has three practices, which focus on managing the involvement of stakeholders to satisfy commitments and resolve misunderstandings, tracking critical project dependencies, and resolving outstanding coordination issues.

The addition of IPPD adds one more specific goal: manage the project using IPPD principles (see Figure 7-11). This goal, which is dubbed SG 3, creates an environment for integrated teams to be effective. The first specific practice establishes and maintains a shared vision for the

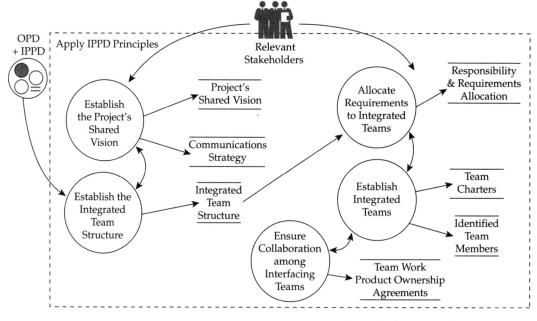

© 2008 by Carnegie Mellon University.

Figure 7-11: *Integrated Project Management for IPPD context diagram*

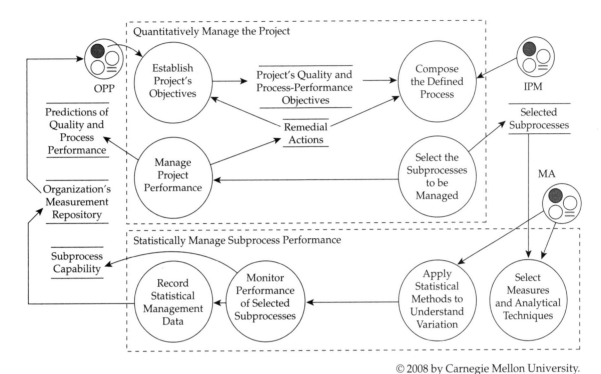

Figure 7-12: *Quantitative Project Management context diagram*

project, together with a strategy for the communication of that vision, including published statements. The subsequent practices focus on organizing integrated teams by determining the appropriate team structure for the project; allocating requirements, responsibilities, and tasks to the teams; establishing the teams; and ensuring that the teams collaborate as appropriate.

7.1.2.4 Quantitative Project Management

The purpose of the Quantitative Project Management process area is to quantitatively manage the project's defined process to achieve the project's established quality and process performance objectives. QPM (see Figure 7-12) has two specific goals that build on the goals of PP, PMC, and IPM: using performance objectives to quantitatively manage the project and statistically managing selected subprocesses. The first goal includes specific practices that establish quality and process-performance objectives, compose the project's defined process based on historical data, select candidate subprocesses that are to be statistically managed, and monitor the project's performance objectives to determine whether they have been satisfied (with corrective actions identified as needed). The specific practices associated with the second goal define statistical management in CMMI. Measures and analytical techniques are selected, statistical methods are applied to understand the natural bounds of variation for subprocess performance, and selected subprocesses are monitored, so that action can be taken to address any deficiencies in process capability. Finally, the resulting data is maintained in a measurement repository for later use throughout the organization. In this way, QPM expands an existing measurement program (following PMC) with the addition of statistical management techniques.

7.1.2.5 Risk Management

The purpose of Risk Management is to identify potential problems before they occur, so that risk-handling activities may be planned and invoked as needed across the life cycle to mitigate adverse impacts on achieving objectives.[10] RSKM (see Figure 7-13) actually builds on part of the PP process area; that is, a specific practice in PP identifies and analyzes project risks, and the project plan should document those risks. Nevertheless, PP is less systematic and less proactive than the requirements noted in RSKM. Often RSKM is applied outside the project context to manage organizational risks. Several other process areas also reference RSKM.

RSKM has three specific goals that focus on preparation for risk management, identification and analysis of the risks, and handling and mitigation of risks as appropriate. The preparation steps include determining risk sources and the categories used for organizing risks by "bins," establishing the parameters used to analyze and categorize risks, and developing a risk strategy. The identification and analysis steps focus on identifying risks, and then ranking them based on the analysis parameters. The handling and mitigation of the risks involves developing, implementing and updating risk mitigation plans.

---

10. At the present time, many organizations consider risk management and opportunity management to be two sides of the same coin. That is, they coordinate efforts to identify potential problems with efforts to identify potential opportunities. While they are working to mitigate adverse effects on achieving objectives, these organizations may also work to take advantage of changes that would help them to achieve their objectives. By realizing an opportunity, the level associated with a related risk may be reduced. Of course, CMMI emphasizes identifying opportunities for improvement of processes and capitalizing on the ability to respond to business opportunities. Currently, however, CMMI does not systematically link the management of risks and opportunities.

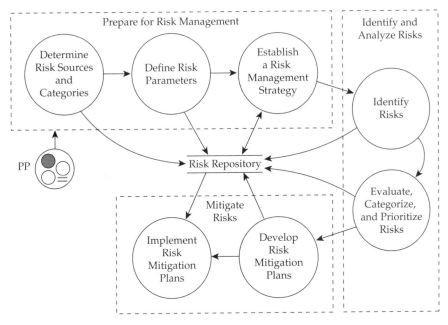

© 2008 by Carnegie Mellon University.

Figure 7-13: *Risk Management context diagram*

7.1.3 Foundation Engineering Process Areas

The CMMI foundation includes one Engineering process area: Requirements Management (REQM).[11] REQM is in the foundation because all projects should have requirements and should manage them whether or not they develop products.

7.1.3.1 Requirements Management

The purpose of Requirements Management is to manage the requirements of the project's products and product components and to identify inconsistencies between those requirements and the project's plans and work products. REQM (see Figure 7-14) has one specific goal: to manage requirements and identify inconsistencies with plans and work products. It is the only Engineering process area that is staged at ML 2; all other process areas are staged at ML 3.[12]

---

11. The CMMI-ACQ model does not contain the Engineering category. REQM is included in the Project Management category in that model.
12. The SW-CMM featured a Requirements Management process area at ML 2 that led to the inclusion of this process area at ML 2 in CMMI.

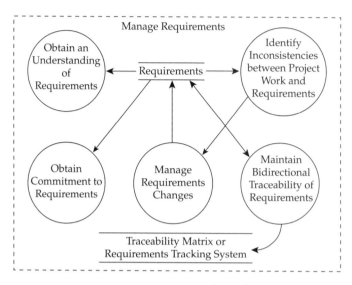

Figure 7-14: *Requirements Management context diagram*

REQM has five specific practices. To manage requirements, the person or team that receives them needs to develop an understanding with the requirement providers of what those requirements mean before doing anything with them. The manager or team should also obtain a commitment from the people who will implement the requirements. Once the requirements are received and understood, and a commitment is obtained, all changes to the requirements should be managed, including recording change histories and evaluating change impacts. The project should provide for bidirectional traceability of the requirement and the associated work products. Tracing the requirements provides a better basis for determining the ramifications of changes; it also ensures that all requirements have a parent and that the product design covers all high-level requirements. Finally, the project should identify inconsistencies between the requirements and work products. Any corrective action required to fix inconsistencies is accomplished in the requirements development process, the project planning process, or possibly other processes.

7.1.4 Foundation Support Process Areas

The Support process areas provide essential processes that are used by other CMMI process areas; in addition, they are used by the CMMI generic practices. In general, these process areas are primarily targeted toward the project (except for Process and Product Quality Assurance). When necessary, however, they can be applied more generally to the organization. For example, Process and Product Quality Assurance can be used with all other process areas to provide an objective review of the processes and work products described in those process areas.

The CMMI Model Foundation includes five Support process areas:

- Configuration Management (CM)
- Process and Product Quality Assurance (PPQA)
- Measurement and Analysis (MA)
- Causal Analysis and Resolution (CAR)
- Decision Analysis and Resolution (DAR)

7.1.4.1 Configuration Management

The purpose of Configuration Management is to establish and maintain the integrity of work products using configuration identification, configuration control, configuration status accounting, and configuration audits. CM (see Figure 7-15) includes three specific goals that address establishing baselines, tracking and controlling changes, and establishing the integrity of baselines. It is assumed that configuration management can occur at multiple levels of granularity and formality. This process area is closely connected with the CL 2 generic practice to manage configurations; it provides the process to be used when applying that generic practice.

The first goal—establishing baselines for work products—has three specific practices: identifying the items to be placed under configuration management, establishing a configuration management and change management system, and creating and releasing the baselines. Once baselines are established using a configuration management system, all changes are tracked and controlled in the second goal with two specific practices: The first tracks the requests for changes and the second tracks content changes to the configuration items. The third goal—establishing the integrity of the baselines—has two specific practices: one for keeping records on the configuration items, and another for performing configuration audits to ensure that the baselines are correct.

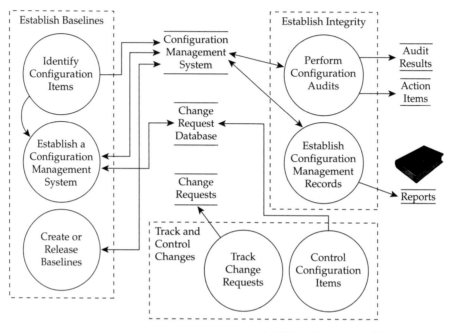

Figure 7-15: *Configuration Management context diagram*

7.1.4.2 Process and Product Quality Assurance

The purpose of Process and Product Quality Assurance is to provide staff and management with objective insight into the processes and associated work products. PPQA (see Figure 7-16) has two specific goals: objectively evaluating adherence to process descriptions, standards, and procedures; and tracking, communicating, and resolving noncompliance issues. To achieve objective evaluation, some organizations may strive for independent oversight of the processes and work products, perhaps via a quality assurance department. Other organizations may embed the quality assurance function within the process, thus placing greater emphasis on evaluation by peers. CMMI supports both options. This process area is closely connected with the generic practice at CL 2 to objectively evaluate adherence; it provides the process to be used when applying that generic practice.

The first goal—objectively evaluating adherence of the performed process and associated work products and services to applicable process descriptions, standards, and procedures—is addressed with

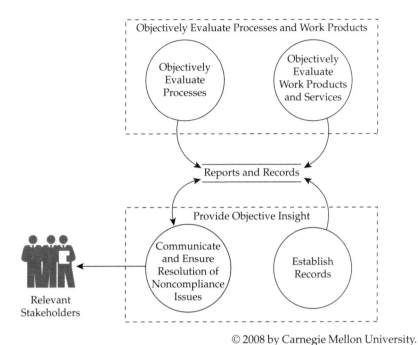

© 2008 by Carnegie Mellon University.

Figure 7-16: *Process and Product Quality Assurance context diagram*

two specific practices. One conducts an objective evaluation of the performed process against the defined process, and the other performs an objective evaluation of designated work products and services. The second goal—tracking, communicating, and resolving noncompliance issues—is also addressed by two specific practices. The first communicates noncompliance issues with relevant stakeholders and ensures their resolution by progressive escalation, and the second establishes and maintains records of quality assurance activities.

7.1.4.3 Measurement and Analysis

The purpose of Measurement and Analysis is to develop and sustain a measurement capability that is used to support management information needs. MA (see Figure 7-17) has two specific goals: one for aligning measurement activities with information needs, and one for providing measurement results that satisfy those needs. This process area is loosely connected with two generic practices at CL 2. That is, *planning the process* includes defining measurement objectives, and *monitoring and controlling* the process encompasses measuring performance against

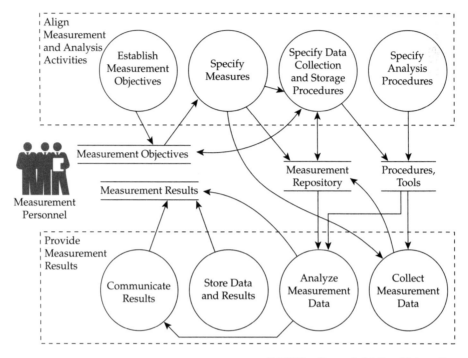

© 2008 by Carnegie Mellon University.

Figure 7-17: *Measurement and Analysis context diagram*

the plan. MA is most successful when the information needs are tied to the organization's business goals and objectives.

The practices of the two MA goals provide an eight-step measurement process, in which four specific practices are mapped to each of the two goals. For the first goal, personnel define the objectives to meet the information needs, specify the measures that will be needed to meet the objectives, indicate how the data will be obtained and stored, and determine how the data will be analyzed and reported. For the second goal, they collect the data, analyze and interpret the data, manage and store both the data and the analysis results, and communicate the results to the stakeholders.[13]

---

13. The Measurement and Analysis process area in CMMI is closely aligned with ISO/IEC 15939:2007 (Systems and Software Engineering—Measurement Process).

7.1.4.4 Decision Analysis and Resolution

The purpose of Decision Analysis and Resolution is to analyze possible decisions using a formal evaluation process that evaluates identified alternatives against established criteria. DAR (see Figure 7-18) has one specific goal, related to evaluating alternatives using established criteria. Only the key issues for a project would warrant the structured decision-making process of DAR. Possible examples include architectural or design alternatives, make-versus-buy decisions, supplier selection, and tool selection.

The practices of this process area identify a six-step process for making decisions in a structured manner:

1. Establish and maintain guidelines to determine which issues are subject to a formal evaluation process.
2. Establish and maintain the criteria for evaluating alternatives as well as the relative ranking of these criteria.
3. Identify alternative solutions to address issues.
4. Select the evaluation methods.[14]

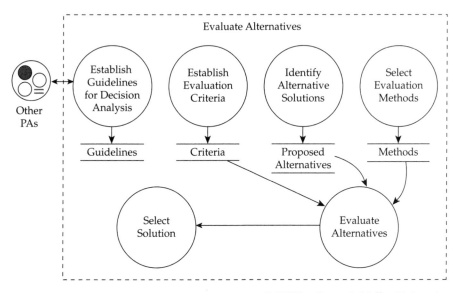

© 2008 by Carnegie Mellon University.

Figure 7-18: *Decision Analysis and Resolution context diagram*

---

14. Examples of methods may include using models and simulations, making estimates, conducting experiments or studies, running tests, obtaining supplier data, or soliciting user reviews.

5. Evaluate alternative solutions using the established criteria and methods.

6. Select a solution, documenting its results and rationale.

An organization may use DAR for any significant decision that needs to be made. Typically, this occurs in the following circumstances: (1) a customer requires it; (2) the decision relates to a high-risk item or would have a significant effect on costs or schedule; (3) a contract modification might result from the decision; (4) there is substantial stakeholder disagreement on the issue; or (5) the decision may be the subject of a future audit. As a part of the decision-making process, stakeholders can provide much of the needed information. A trade study for making important technical decisions is an example of a formal DAR process. Because following a DAR process expends resources, it should not be used for making decisions with little project impact or little associated risk. In reality, some process is used even in low-level decisions; such a process just isn't required or expected by the CMMI models.[15]

7.1.4.5 Causal Analysis and Resolution

The purpose of Causal Analysis and Resolution is to identify causes of defects and other problems and take action to prevent them from occurring in the future. CAR (see Figure 7-19) has two specific goals: one for determining the root causes of defects, and another for addressing these causes to prevent their future occurrence. This process area is closely related to the CL 5 generic practice concerning the root causes of defects and other process-related problems; the processes of CAR should be used when applying that generic practice.[16]

For the first goal (determining root causes), two specific practices exist: select the defects for analysis, and perform causal analysis and propose actions to address these problems. For the second goal (addressing the root causes of defects and other problems), three specific practices are

---

15. The Decision Management Process that is defined in ISO/IEC 15288:2008 (6.3.3) and ISO/IEC 12207:2008 (6.3.3) is very similar to is the process specified in CMMI. To comply with the ISO/IEC standards, however, a project must also confirm that the decision was effective, which is not called out in CMMI.

16. Sometimes people are surprised that CAR is staged at ML 5 in CMMI. Obviously, finding and fixing root causes of defects and other problems is a major activity within most successful projects. In fact, some of the members of the first CMMI team thought that CAR should be staged at ML 2, but the final decision placed it at ML 5. The primary reason for this decision was its use to evaluate the effects of changes on process performance. Some causal analysis methods may actually identify problems before they ever occur, thereby avoiding the possibility of problem processes being deployed. Nonetheless, you may start to think about CAR-related activities at lower maturity levels.

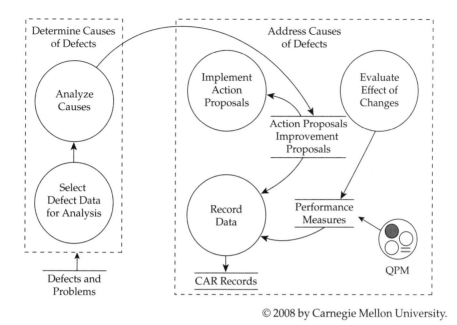

Figure 7-19: *Causal Analysis and Resolution context diagram*

provided: implement the action proposals, evaluate the effects of the changes on process performance, and record the data from the CAR activities for subsequent use by other projects in the organization.

7.2 Development Constellation

7.2.1 Development Engineering Process Areas

In both the Process Management category and the Project Management category, (some of) the process areas build upon and presuppose others. In contrast, the Engineering category lacks one-directional, "build upon" relationships between process areas. Instead, it is assumed that all of the process areas are used together in an integrated manner. In CMMI, the Engineering process areas form a "product-oriented" set of process areas. Improving product development processes means targeting essential business objectives, rather than the more narrow objectives of specific disciplines. That is, the Engineering process areas are constructed to discourage the tendency toward a "stovepiped" set of processes.

The Engineering process areas apply to the development of any product or service in the engineering development domain (e.g., systems, software products, hardware products, services, or processes). These process areas address development of a "product" rather than a "system"—a choice in terminology that allows the process areas to apply recursively at all levels of product development. Thus the term "product component" designates the building blocks of the "product."[17]

These process areas are constructed to apply to many different types of organizations, not just those responsible for the initial systems engineering, hardware engineering, and software engineering. For example, a software maintenance organization that provides software updates to a system may not have been part of the initial development effort. Such a group may review the CMMI Engineering process areas and decide that Requirements Development doesn't apply to it; someone else handled those activities. In reality, any engineering change request is based on some need. That need should be elicited, new requirements should be determined based on it, and alternative solutions should be considered before the selected solution is designed, implemented, verified, and validated. In this way, the technical control based on these principles ensures that all maintenance actions are necessary and meet the user's needs.

Five Engineering process areas exist in the Development constellation:

- Requirements Development (RD)
- Technical Solution (TS)
- Product Integration (PI)
- Verification (VER)
- Validation (VAL)

7.2.1.1 Requirements Development

The purpose of Requirements Development is to produce and analyze customer, product, and product component requirements. RD (see Figure 7-20) has three specific goals: developing customer requirements, developing product requirements, and analyzing and validating requirements

---

17. Those using ISO/IEC 15288 will recognize that the terminology in this international standard differs from what is used in CMMI. ISO/IEC 15288 (Systems Engineering—System Life Cycle Processes) describes "systems," "system elements," "systems-of-interest," and "enabling systems," which make up the basic terminological framework. For example, a system element from one perspective may be a system-of-interest from another perspective.

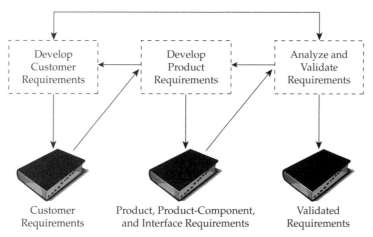

© 2008 by Carnegie Mellon University.

Figure 7-20: *Requirements Development context diagram*

to produce a definition of the required functionality. This process area contains all of the practices related to generating product and product component requirements. It is recursive relative to TS, with alternative solutions being developed to help determine lower-level product requirements.

Figure 7-20 shows a simplified context diagram for RD, because this process area contains too many specific practices to include in one diagram. Furthermore, Figure 7-20 does not really illustrate how the requirements are developed. The analysis tasks are performed concurrently with the development tasks. Processes developed from RD practices should be designed to meet the needs of the organization, and can represent several different product life-cycle models, such as waterfall, iterative, incremental, and multilevel models.

The development process needs a starting point, and RD's first goal provides it by developing customer requirements. The first specific practice calls for the elicitation of stakeholder needs, expectations, constraints, and interfaces. Providing information about needs allows the customer (and other stakeholders) to describe the product's desired function, performance, appearance, and other characteristics. In the second specific practice, the stakeholders' needs, expectations, constraints, and interfaces are translated into customer requirements.

RD's second goal addresses the use of customer requirements to develop the product-level and product-component-level requirements.

In some cases, these requirements may consist of a system and its sub-systems, boxes, boards, software configuration items, software components, and modules. In other cases, they may include processes, subprocesses, or service-related products. The three specific practices for this goal focus on translating the customer requirements into the more technical form of product requirements, allocating the requirements to each component of the product, and identifying interface requirements. One way of handling interfaces is to treat them as if they were the same as the other requirements. Note, however, that a lack of attention to the interfaces often results in defects, which can ultimately lead to rework, cost overruns, and schedule slips.[18]

In RD's third goal, the requirements are analyzed and validated as they are developed; this step is critical for the success of a product. The five specific practices that map to this goal involve preparation, analysis, and validation. The specific practices begin with the development of operational concepts and scenarios that detail the way the product will be used, stored, transported, and so forth. These operational concepts then help define the requirements from a broad, in-use point of view, and they establish a definition of the required functionality. Analysis of the requirements ensures that they are necessary and sufficient to meet the objectives of the higher-level requirements and that they are feasible to achieve. In addition, requirements are analyzed to balance stakeholder needs and constraints. The last specific practice addresses requirements validation, which ensures that the resulting product will perform appropriately in its intended use environment.

7.2.1.2 Technical Solution

The purpose of Technical Solution is to develop, design, and implement solutions to requirements. Solutions, designs, and implementations encompass products, product components, and product-related life-cycle processes, either singly or in combinations as appropriate. TS (see Figure 7-21) has three specific goals that address selecting product component solutions, developing the design, and implementing the design. The high-level context diagram in Figure 7-21 shows only the goals for this process area. In the first goal, alternative solutions are developed and analyzed, and the one that best satisfies the criteria is selected. The selected alternative may be used to develop more detailed requirements in the RD process

---

18. Those who aim to develop systems using a Modular Open Systems Approach (MOSA) need to pay special attention to conformance with standard interfaces that are the key to making the system "open."

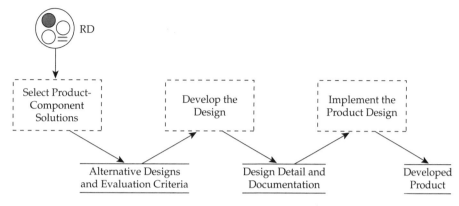

© 2008 by Carnegie Mellon University.

Figure 7-21: *Technical Solution context diagram*

area or designed in the second goal of TS. After the product components are designed, they are implemented together with support documentation in the third goal of TS.

The first TS goal includes two specific practices. First, the project must develop alternative solutions, as well as criteria for their evaluation. Alternatives are explored to determine the best solution for the product or product component. In some cases, this investigation may result in additional requirements or lead to modification of existing requirements. This activity is usually recursive with the requirements development processes. In the second specific practice, the engineer or team selects the solution that best satisfies the established criteria.

Four specific practices are associated with the second TS goal (developing the product or product component designs). The first practice develops an architecture and a design for the product or product components. These are characterized (in the second specific practice) by means of a technical data package. The third specific practice establishes product component interface solutions, and does so in terms of established criteria. In the fourth specific practice, the project evaluates whether the product components should be developed, purchased, or reused. If the decision is made to purchase a component, the SAM process area establishes the agreement and manages it.

The third TS goal (implementing the product components and generating associated support documentation) has two specific practices. For the first, the project implements the designs for all types of product components—software, hardware, and so on. For the second, it develops and maintains the end-use support documentation that describes how to install, operate, and maintain the product.

7.2.1.3 Product Integration

The purpose of Product Integration is to assemble the product from the product components; ensure that the product, as integrated, functions properly; and deliver the product. PI (see Figure 7-22) has three specific goals that address preparing for integration, ensuring interface compatibility, and assembling the product components for delivery.

The first goal—preparing for integration—includes three specific practices. First, the project develops the sequence for integration, which assists in the overall planning effort. Second, it establishes the environment for integration. Finally, it defines the procedures and criteria for integration.

The second goal—ensuring that the interfaces (both internal and external) are compatible—has two specific practices. First, the project reviews

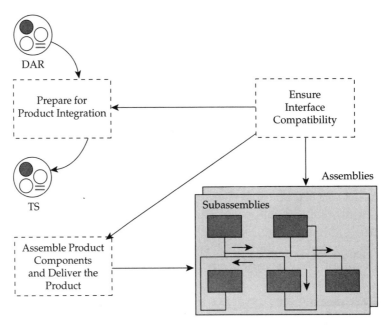

© 2008 by Carnegie Mellon University.

Figure 7-22: *Product Integration context diagram*

the interface descriptions for coverage and completeness. Note that interfaces to the environment are included in this practice. Then, the project manages the interface definitions, designs, and changes for the product and product components to maintain consistency and resolve issues.

Four specific practices exist for the third goal—verifying that product components are assembled and that the integrated, verified, and validated product is delivered. After the product components are implemented and unit testing is complete, the integration process begins. The lowest levels of the product are usually integrated first, with the product being assembled in successive stages. In the CMMI, the delivery of the product occurs in the PI process area. First, the project confirms that each component has been properly identified and functions according to its description and that the interfaces comply with their descriptions. This step helps the engineering team avoid problems during assembly of the product components, which occurs in the second specific practice. In the third specific practice, personnel evaluate the assembly according to the procedures, focusing on interface compatibility. Finally, they package the product and deliver it to the appropriate customer.[19]

7.2.1.4 Verification

The purpose of Verification is to assure that selected work products meet their specified requirements. VER (see Figure 7-23) has three specific goals that address preparing for verification, performing peer reviews on selected work products, and verifying selected work products.

The three specific practices for the first goal regarding verification preparation resemble the specific practices of PI: select the work products to be verified and the verification methods early in the project, establish and maintain the environment for verification, and define the verification procedures and criteria for selected work products. Verification planning is performed early in the project, because many of the activities associated with requirements development and design (such as analyses, reviews, and demonstrations) involve ensuring that the requirements are, in fact, verifiable.

Three practices are included for the peer review goal. Peer reviews are a specialized verification activity intended to reduce defects in selected

---

19. It may take some inspired interpretation to apply this particular set of practices to an agile life cycle where integration is continuous. However, nothing prevents such an approach.

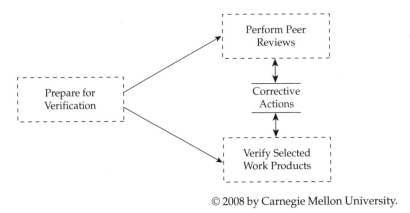

Figure 7-23: *Verification context diagram*

work products. Among software developers, they have proven to be a highly valuable technique, and interest in their use by other engineering disciplines seems to be growing. For the specific practices, the project first prepares for the peer reviews (what gets reviewed, by whom, when, and using which review criteria), then conducts those reviews, and finally analyzes the results. Selecting what gets reviewed is a critical step in the preparation stage; the resources needed for conducting the reviews mean that they should remain limited to key work products.[20]

For the third goal of verifying selected work products, two specific practices exist. First, personnel perform verification according to the verification procedures, capturing results and associated action items. Then, they analyze the results and identify any needed corrective actions based on established verification criteria.

7.2.1.5 Validation

The purpose of Validation is to demonstrate that a product or product component fulfills its intended use when placed in its intended environment. VAL (see Figure 7-24) has two specific goals that address preparing for validation, and then validating the product or product components. Although the validation practices are similar to those used in verification, the two process areas focus on importantly different topics. Vali-

---

20. In our experience, a schedule may end up with many peer reviews planned for about the same time—namely, immediately prior to a formal review with, or a delivery to, a customer. This becomes a major challenge because the "peers" who need to find time to conduct a review on the work of others are very busy trying to complete their own work. Be sure to take this issue into account when creating schedules, or your peer reviews may have very limited value.

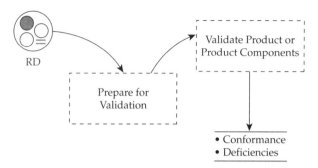

Figure 7-24: *Validation context diagram*

dation addresses those activities needed to show that a product fulfills its intended use in its intended environment; verification ensures the work products meet their specified requirements.[21] An examination of the product in use may show that some of the requirements were not adequately captured.

The goal of preparing for validation has three specific practices, which mirror those in PI and VER. First, the project selects the products and product components for validation, together with the validation methods. Next, it establishes the environment for validation. Finally, personnel define the procedures and criteria for validation.

The goal of actually performing the validation has two specific practices. First, workers perform the validation according to the procedures to show that the product or product component performs as intended. Then, they capture and analyze the validation results, identifying any problems or unresolved issues regarding intended use or operational need.

7.2.2 Development Project Management Process Areas

One project management process exists in the Development constellation: Supplier Agreement Management (SAM). SAM is included in this constellation because it focuses on the procurement of product components for the product being developed. SAM is more closely associated with the Engineering process areas than with the other project management process areas—a relationship that is readily evident when we

---

21. As the old adage goes, you verify that you built the product right and validate that it was the right product.

note how the specific practices in SAM largely parallel the specific practices of the Engineering process areas.

7.2.2.1 Supplier Agreement Management

The purpose of Supplier Agreement Management is to manage the acquisition of products from suppliers. SAM (see Figure 7-25) has two specific goals: one for establishing supplier agreements, and another for satisfying those agreements. This process area works in cooperation with the TS process area, in which the organization faces the make-versus-buy decision. Once a decision to buy is made, SAM creates the agreement and then manages it from the viewpoint of the developer who is acquiring the component. Product component requirements for the items being acquired are developed in the Requirements Development process area.[22]

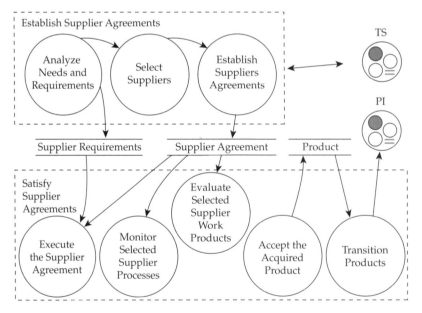

© 2008 by Carnegie Mellon University.

Figure 7-25: *Supplier Agreement Management context diagram*

---

22. Two of the SAM specific practices were inherited from a process area that existed in the now-superseded version 1.1 of CMMI: Integrated Supplier Management (ISM).

To establish supplier agreements (the first SAM goal), the project analyzes and selects the acquisition options to be followed. These could include an external contract, an internal vendor, a customer-supplied item, or use of commercial-off-the-shelf products. Suppliers are then identified and selected, based on project-related criteria. A DAR process may be followed when there are multiple potential suppliers. Once the selection is made, an agreement is established.

To satisfy those supplier agreements (the second SAM goal), the project (as the acquirer) performs the activities specified in the supplier agreements. These include monitoring supplier progress and performance, conducting reviews, and monitoring risks. To make potential issues visible as early as possible, the project selects and monitors critical supplier processes, especially ones that relate to components with key interfaces.[23] The project evaluates any custom-made work products from the supplier, and conducts acceptance reviews, tests, and configuration audits. Finally, to ensure an easy transition into the project integration effort, appropriate steps are followed to receive, store, and maintain the acquired products.

7.3 Acquisition Constellation Process Areas

7.3.1 Acquisition Process Areas

The Acquisition constellation addresses the practices associated with the acquirer side of product procurement. Five specific practices were added to four CMF Project Management process areas—PP, PMC, IPM, and OPD.[24] A new category called Acquisition contains six process areas that address aspects of both engineering and project management:

- Agreement Management (AM)—ML 2
- Acquisition Requirements Development (ARD)—ML 2[25]

---

23. The extent to which process monitoring is appropriate will depend on many factors, such as the past performance of the supplier in producing similar components and the risks associated with the development.

24. In each of these four process areas, one or more specific practices has been added to address key topics—for example, establishing an acquisition strategy (PP); planning and monitoring the transition to operations and support of acquired products (PP and PMC); establishing integrated teams (IPM); and establishing rules and guidelines for integrated teams (OPD).

25. Unlike Requirements Development that in CMMI-DEV is staged at maturity level 3, Acquisition Requirements Development is staged at maturity level 2 in CMMI-ACQ.

- Acquisition Technical Management (ATM)—ML 3
- Acquisition Validation (AVAL)—ML 3
- Acquisition Verification (AVER)—ML 3
- Solicitation and Supplier Agreement Development (SSAD)—ML 2

Acquisition management is covered in the CMF project management process areas, as well as in three of these six process areas—SSAD, AM, and ATM. SSAD addresses the solicitation practices and the development of the agreement. While it is similar to SAM, SG 1 (in the Development constellation), SSAD focuses on the acquirer's key activities to reach an agreement. Once the agreement is in place, the AM process area addresses the management of the contract. It has similarities to SAM, SG 2. ATM addresses interfaces and the selection and management of technical reviews.

Acquisition technical activities are covered in the other three process areas—ARD, AVAL, and AVER. Some of the specific practices are identical to or largely duplicate the specific practices from the corresponding DEV process areas, whereas others are modified to better address acquirer practices.

7.3.1.1 Agreement Management

The purpose of Agreement Management is to ensure that the supplier and the acquirer perform according to the terms of the supplier agreement. AM (see Figure 7-26) has one specific goal, dealing with having the agreement met by both the acquirer and the supplier. AM works in cooperation with other project management process areas to ensure that the project is managed such that suppliers are considered a key part of the overall project.

Managing supplier agreements includes four specific practices. The first specific practice has the acquirer doing the things that it signed up for in the supplier agreement, including monitoring the project progress of the supplier and any subsequent corrective actions. The second specific practice addresses managing selected critical supplier processes with an eye toward achieving early awareness of potential problems and preventing interface problems. The acceptance by the acquirer of the acquired product or service is the third specific practice, ensuring (in conjunction with stakeholders) that all of the requirements have

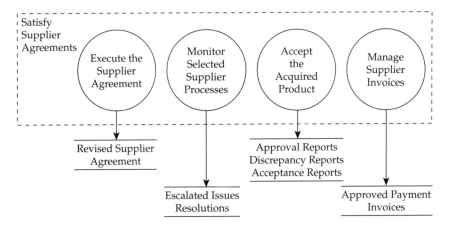

Figure 7-26: *Agreement Management context diagram*

been met. The last specific practice involves managing invoices to ensure that all payment terms have been satisfied.

7.3.1.2 Acquisition Requirements Development

The purpose of Acquisition Requirements Development is to develop and analyze customer and contractual requirements. ARD (see Figure 7-27) has three specific goals: developing customer requirements, developing contractual requirements, and analyzing and validating the requirements. ARD works in cooperation with AVER and AVAL to engineer the product being acquired. A close relationship also exists between ARD and SSAD, thereby ensuring that the requirements defined in the solicitation and specified in the agreement are correct.

Developing customer requirements includes the elicitation of stakeholder needs, expectations, constraints, and interfaces, plus their subsequent transformation into customer requirements. Developing contractual requirements in the supplier agreement includes establishing and maintaining contractual requirements based on the customer requirements, and allocating contractual requirements for each supplier deliverable. The analysis and validation activities include establishing and maintaining operational concepts and scenarios, ensuring that the contractual requirements are necessary and sufficient, analyzing

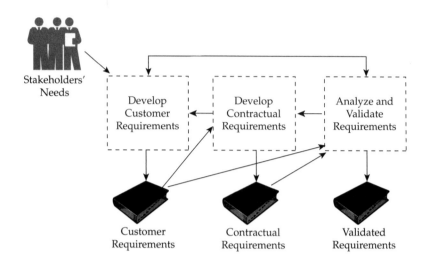

© 2008 by Carnegie Mellon University.

Figure 7-27: *Acquisition Requirements Development context diagram*

risks so as to balance stakeholder needs and constraints, and validating contractual requirements to confirm that the resulting product will perform as intended in the user's environment.

7.3.1.3 Acquisition Technical Management

The purpose of Acquisition Technical Management is to evaluate the supplier's technical solution and to manage selected interfaces of that solution. ATM (see Figure 7-28) has two specific goals: one to address the evaluation of technical solutions developed by the supplier, and one to perform interface management. This process area works in cooperation with ARD, AVER, and AVAL to manage the product being acquired.

The goal for evaluating technical solutions has three specific practices. The first specific practice selects supplier technical solutions for analysis and the methods to be used; the second performs the analysis, holding technical interchange meetings as needed; and the third conducts technical reviews to confirm that products and services will meet user needs and requirements. These reviews, which are defined in the supplier agreement and are intended to improve the supplier's technical solution, are event-driven milestones in the development process.

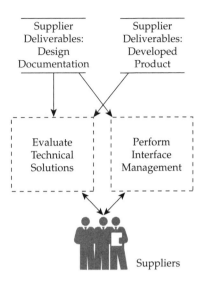

Figure 7-28: *Acquisition Technical Management context diagram*

The second goal for ATM has two specific practices: one selects the interfaces that will be managed, and the other performs the interface management. By focusing on the interfaces, transition and integration problems may be avoided.

7.3.1.4 Acquisition Validation

The purpose of Acquisition Validation is to demonstrate that an acquired product or service fulfills its intended use when placed in its intended environment. AVAL (see Figure 7-29) has two specific goals: to prepare for validation, and to validate the products or services. This process area works in cooperation with ARD and AVER to develop the product being acquired.

The goal of preparing for validation has three specific practices, which mirror those in AVER. First, the project selects the products and product components for validation and identifies the validation methods. Next, it establishes and maintains the environment for validation, addressing resources and their availability. Finally, it defines the procedures and criteria for validation, keeping them current as the product or service matures.

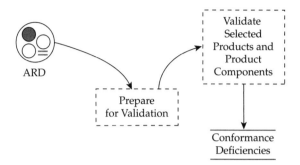

Figure 7-29: *Acquisition Validation context diagram*

The goal of actually performing the validation has two specific practices. First, workers perform the validation according to the procedures to show that the product or product component performs as intended. Then, they capture and analyze the validation results, identifying any problems or unresolved issues. Note that this process area closely mirrors the VAL process area within CMMI-DEV (see Section 7.2.1.5).

7.3.1.5 Acquisition Verification

The purpose of Acquisition Verification is to assure that selected work products meet their specified requirements. AVER (see Figure 7-30) has three specific goals that address preparing for verification, performing peer reviews, and verifying selected work products.

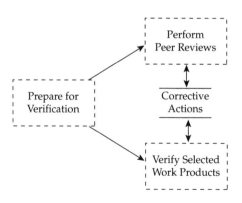

Figure 7-30: *Acquisition Verification context diagram*

The three specific practices for the first goal (preparing for verification) resemble the AVAL specific practices: select the acquirer work products and the verification methods early in the project, establish and maintain the environment for verification, and define the procedures and criteria for selected acquirer work products. Verification planning is performed early in the project, as many of the activities associated with requirements development and design (such as conducting analyses, reviews, and demonstrations) focus on ensuring that the requirements are, in fact, verifiable.

The three practices included in the second goal (performing peer reviews) are almost identical to those in the CMMI-DEV version of VER. See Section 7.2.1.4 for a description of these practices.

For the third goal (verifying selected work products), two specific practices exist. First, personnel perform verification according to the verification procedures, capturing results and associated action items. Then, they analyze the results and identify corrective actions based on established verification criteria. As was the case with AVAL, AVER closely mirrors the VER process area within CMMI-DEV.

7.3.1.6 Solicitation and Supplier Agreement Development

The purpose of Solicitation and Supplier Agreement Development is to prepare a solicitation package, select one or more suppliers to deliver the product or service, and establish and maintain the supplier agreement. SSAD (see Figure 7-31) has three specific goals that exactly mirror this purpose statement: to prepare for the solicitation and supplier agreement development, to select suppliers, and to establish and maintain the supplier agreements.

To prepare for solicitation and supplier agreement development there are four specific practices: potential suppliers are identified, a solicitation package is developed, that package is reviewed to ensure realism, and finally it is distributed and maintained throughout the solicitation. To select suppliers using a formal evaluation, the acquirer selection policies and procedures are followed: proposals from suppliers are evaluated, negotiation plans are developed for each supplier, and after negotiations the suppliers are selected with the results documented. Finally, the supplier agreements are established and maintained by creating a mutual understanding of the agreement between the suppliers and the acquirer, and then documenting and maintaining the agreement.

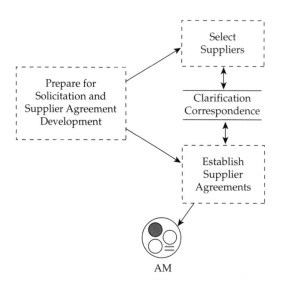

Figure 7-31: *Solicitation and Supplier Agreement Development context diagram*

7.4 Services Constellation Process Areas[26]

The Services constellation addresses the establishment, management, and delivery of services, where a service is defined as an intangible, nonstorable product. The CMMI for Services (CMMI-SVC) constellation includes the 16 foundation process areas, one of which (Requirements Management) contains an addition to address requirements for service agreements. It also includes Supplier Agreement Management from the Development constellation, five other required process areas, and three additions (optional process areas). Amplifications for Services have been added to six process areas: CM, PMC, PP, PPQA, RSKM, and SAM.

---

26. At the time of this book's publication, the Services constellation was in draft form and discussions were ongoing as to how to include its information in the CMMI Product Suite. Even though there may be significant changes between the material presented here and any released versions, the authors felt it was important to include this work-in-progress as information to service-providing organizations and to encourage feedback from the services community. Context diagrams are not shown for these process areas.

The required process areas addressed in this section are as follows:

- Capacity and Availability Management (CAM)
- Requirements Management (REQM +SVC)
- Problem Management (PRM)
- Incident and Request Management (IRM)
- Service Delivery (SD)
- Service Transition (ST)

The additions (optional process areas) addressed in this section are as follows:

- Organizational Service Management (OSM)
- Service Continuity (SCON)
- Service System Development (SSD)

The Services constellation makes no use of the Engineering process area category that is a part of CMMI-DEV, and no use of the Acquisition category that is a part of CMMI-ACQ. Instead, the process areas IRM, SD, SDD, and ST constitute a Service Establishment and Delivery category.

The additions provide various options for the content of Services models depending on the organizational business context. The following list shows the combinations of model components that could be used:

- CMMI-SVC
- CMMI-SVC+OSM
- CMMI-SVC+SCON
- CMMI-SVC+SSD
- CMMI-SVC+OSM+SCON
- CMMI-SVC+OSM+SSD
- CMMI-SVC+SCON+SSD
- CMMI-SVC+OSM+SCON+SSD

7.4.1 Services Process Management Process Areas

7.4.1.1 Organizational Service Management (Addition)

The purpose of Organizational Service Management is to establish and maintain standard services that ensure the satisfaction of the organization's customer base. OSM has two specific goals: one to address long-term customer satisfaction, and one to establish and maintain standard services for the organization. Note that OSM is an optional process area in the Services constellation.

To address long-term customer satisfaction, data is gathered about customer satisfaction and the alignment between customer needs and standard services. Subsequently, this data is analyzed to identify opportunities for improvements to the standard services. The needs of the organization's customers are translated into decisions about which services will be developed.

To establish and maintain the organization's standard services, the organization defines the set of services and service levels that will be used, approves descriptions of the services that are approved for use, and establishes and maintains both tailoring guidelines and a service repository. In addition to housing services, levels, descriptions, and tailoring guidelines, the service repository may contain related information, such as sales instructions, and lists of proposal authors and contract specialists.

This process area is similar in concept to the OPM process area. Some of the successful practices for these two process areas may be combined within the organization.

7.4.2 Services Project Management Process Areas

7.4.2.1 Capacity and Availability Management

The purpose of Capacity and Availability Management is to plan and monitor the effective provision of resources to support service requirements. CAM has two specific goals: preparing for capability and availability management, and analyzing and monitoring both capacity and availability to manage resources and demand. This process area promotes the proactive management of current and future capacity. The first goal prepares for capacity and availability management by establishing and maintaining a strategy regarding the short-term and long-term use of resources; selecting measures, tools, and analytic techniques to support the management objectives; and collecting data to establish the service's baselines and models. The second goal analyzes and monitors both capacity and availability by looking to the use of resources and services on an ongoing basis, monitoring availability against agreed-upon targets, and reporting relevant data to stakeholders.

7.4.2.2 Service Continuity (Addition)

The purpose of Service Continuity is to establish and maintain contingency plans for continuity of agreed services during and following any significant disruption of normal operations. SCON has three specific goals: to identify and prioritize essential functions, to establish and maintain the service continuity plan, and to validate the effectiveness of the service continuity plan. This process area addresses practices that help an organization continue to deliver services when its normal operations are interrupted. Note that SCON is an optional process area in the Services constellation.

The specific practices for the first goal (identify and prioritize essential functions) are identifying the organization's essential functions to ensure service continuity, identifying internal and external dependencies and interdependencies that the organization relies on to provide services, and identifying vital records and databases, key personnel, responsibilities, and needed protections for the service.

The specific practices for the second goal (establish and maintain the service continuity plan) are developing a plan that (if needed) would enable the organization to continue to provide agreed-to services in the face of threats and vulnerabilities, documenting the tests used to validate the effectiveness of this plan, developing training materials and delivery methods in consultation with stakeholders, and maintaining the plan to address changing needs.

The specific practices for the third goal (to validate the effectiveness of the service continuity plan) are training personnel on the service continuity plan, preparing and conducting validation tests, and, based on an evaluation of testing results, identifying areas for corrective action.

7.4.3 Services Engineering Process Areas

7.4.3.1 Requirements Management +SVC

The purpose of Requirements Management +SVC is the same as the foundation process area's purpose, with an additional purpose statement for services: *REQM also establishes and maintains written agreements between service providers and customers on service requirements and service levels.* (See Section 7.1.3.1 for REQM as a foundation process area.) REQM +SVC has one additional specific goal: establish and maintain service requirements agreements. To achieve this goal, the specific practices have members of the organization analyzing and comparing existing agreements and service data against the requested requirements, and then establishing and maintaining the service requirements agreement, making it available to service providers and customers, and reviewing it as appropriate to create a revised agreement as needed.

7.4.4 Services Support Process Areas

7.4.4.1 Problem Management

The purpose of Problem Management is to prevent incidents from recurring by identifying and addressing underlying causes of incidents. PM has two specific goals: conducting preparation for problem management and identifying and addressing problems.

The goal of preparation for problem management includes specific practices on establishing and maintaining both a strategy and a system for recording problem information. A strategy is not a detailed plan to address an individual problem; rather, the strategy for problem management addresses at—a high level of responsibility—problem reporting, as well as the methods and tools to be used for problem management.

The goal of addressing problems includes specific practices on identifying and recording problems; analyzing, reviewing, and addressing those problems; monitoring problem resolution and (if needed) escalating a problem for increased attention; and communicating problem status, thereby validating that all problems have been resolved.

7.4.5 Service Establishment and Delivery Process Areas

7.4.5.1 Incident and Request Management

The purpose of Incident and Request Management is to ensure the timely resolution of requests for service and incidents that occur during service delivery. IRM has two specific goals: preparation for and management of incidents and requests. Incidents are defined as interruptions of the agreed-upon level of service. Requests come from customers, who ask the organization to deliver part of a previously agreed-upon service. This definition includes on-demand requests, such as a query for information or data at any point in time.

Preparation for incidents and requests is addressed by creating and maintaining a strategy and a management system for incidents and requests. This sets the stage for managing them in the next goal.

Management of incidents and requests is addressed by identifying and recording them in the management system; analyzing, reviewing, and managing them; monitoring their resolution; and communicating their status with the submitters.

7.4.5.2 Service Delivery

The purpose of Service Delivery is to deliver services in accordance with service agreements. SD has two specific goals: prepare for service delivery and deliver the services.

Preparation for service delivery is accomplished by preparing a service delivery operational plan and preparing the service systems for delivery. Service systems are developed in the SSD process area (an optional process area discussed in Section 7.4.5.3).

Services are delivered by confirming that the appropriate service systems operate as intended in the environment, consumables as needed to provide the service are acquired, services are delivered in accordance with the delivery plan and are monitored, and the service systems are maintained to ensure continuing service delivery.

7.4.5.3 Service System Development (Addition)

The purpose of Service System Development is to analyze, design, develop, integrate, and test service systems to satisfy existing or anticipated service agreements. SSD has three specific goals: develop and analyze service requirements, develop service systems, and test service systems. Note that SSD is an optional process area in the Services constellation. This process area is similar in nature to the Engineering process areas in the CMMI-DEV model.

The first goal (develop and analyze service requirements) is accomplished by developing stakeholder requirements from needs, expectations, and constraints; refining and elaborating those stakeholder requirements so as to develop service and service system requirements; and developing the service system functionality based on the validated requirements.

The second goal (develop service systems) is accomplished by selecting service system solutions from alternatives, developing the designs for service system components, managing internal and external interface definitions and designs, implementing the designs (including the development of end-user documentation), and assembling and integrating the components into the service system.

The third goal (test service systems) is accomplished by establishing and maintaining an approach and an environment for verification and validation, performing peer reviews on selected components, verifying components against their requirements, and validating the service delivery capabilities to ensure that they will meet stakeholder expectations.

7.4.5.4 Service Transition

The purpose of Service Transition is to deploy new or significantly changed service systems while managing their effect on ongoing service delivery. ST has three specific goals: preparing for service system transition, deploying the service system, and retiring the service system.

Preparing for service system transition includes practices for ensuring the operational functionality and compatibility of the service system in the current operating environment, establishing and maintaining a transition plan, and reviewing that plan with stakeholders to obtain commitments.

Deploying service systems includes practices for establishing and maintaining a baseline, installing the service system in the operational environment, testing the system against operational scenarios, preparing users and service provider personnel for changes in services and the planned service availability, and assessing the effects on stakeholders and delivered services after the system is deployed, including taking corrective action as needed. Installing the service system includes packaging, distribution, integration, and installation of service system components within the operational environment.

Retiring the service system includes practices for planning the removal of the service system from the operational environment, archiving the service system work products as required, and removing the service system from the operational environment.

7.5 Relationships within CMMI Components

You have now been introduced to all of the process areas within the two released models, CMMI-DEV and CMMI-ACQ, and the process areas currently proposed for the CMMI-SVC. We conclude this chapter with a brief look at the role of process areas within the CMMI framework.

The internal references in the CMMI models provide valuable information about how the processes work together in support of continuous improvement objectives. Two major sources of relationships are found in the models: those between process areas and those between process areas and generic practices.

7.5.1 Relationships among Process Areas

Table 7-2 describes the key relationships among process areas by summarizing the references from the "Related Process Areas" section of each process area. The models discuss key relationships between process areas in the categories but don't provide a summary of these discussions. Specific information about relationships between lower-level components, such as specific practices and subpractices, is also included in the models, but a summary at that level is beyond the scope of this book.

Table 7-2: *CMMI-Related Process Areas*

Process Area	*Related Process Areas*
Acquisition Requirements Development	REQM, SSAD, ATM, AVAL, RSKM
Acquisition Technical Management	ARD, DAR, REQM, RSKM, CM, AM
Acquisition Validation	ARD, AM, ATM
Acquisition Verification	AVAL, ARD, ATM, REQM
Agreement Management	PMC, MA, SSAD, AVAL, ATM
Capability and Availability Management	REQM, MA

(continued)

Table 7-2: *CMMI-Related Process Areas (Continued)*

Process Area	Related Process Areas
Causal Analysis and Resolution	QPM, OID, MA
Configuration Management	PP, PMC
Decision Analysis and Resolution	PP, IPM+IPPD, RSKM
Incident and Request Management	REQM+SVC, CAM, CM
Integrated Project Management	PP, PMC, VER, OPD+IPPD, MA
Measurement and Analysis	PP, PMC, CM, RD, REQM, OPD+IPPD, QPM
Organizational Innovation and Deployment	OPF, OPD+IPPM, OPP, OT, MA, IPM +IPPD, DAR
Organizational Process Definition	OPF+IPPD
Organizational Process Focus	OPD+IPPD
Organizational Process Performance	QPM, MA
Organizational Service Management	REQM, SSD, SD, PMC, OPD
Organizational Training	OPD+IPPD, PP, DAR
Problem Management	IRM, CM, CAR, REQM+SVC
Process and Product Quality Assurance	PP, VER
Product Integration	RD, TS, VER, VAL, RSKM, DAR, CM, SAM
Project Planning	RD, REQM, RSKM, TS
Project Monitoring and Control	PP, MA
Quantitative Project Management	PMC, MA, OPP, OPD+IPPM, IPM+IPPD, CAR, OID
Requirements Development	REQM, TS, PI, VER, VAL, RSKM, CM

Process Area	Related Process Areas
Requirements Management +SVC	RD, TS, PP, CM, PMC, RSKM, OSM, SAM
Risk Management	PP, PMC, DAR
Service Continuity	OT, DAR, PP, RSKM, SD
Service Delivery	REQM+SVC, ST, SSD, CM, CAM
Service System Development	DAR, REQM+SVC, ST, OSM
Service Transition	SSD, SD, PM, IRM, CM, CAR
Solicitation and Supplier Agreement Development	PP, MA, ARD, REQM, ATM, AM, DAR
Supplier Agreement Management	PMC, RD, REQM, TS
Technical Solution	RD, VER, DAR, REQM, OID
Validation	RD, TS, VER
Verification	RD, VAL, REQM

We can make several observations after looking at Table 7-2. First, note the strong interrelationship within the Engineering process areas. Not surprisingly, Project Planning and Measurement and Analysis are key to the successful implementation of a variety of process areas.

The references also reveal the fundamental interrelationships within the management processes through the number and type of cross references within the Process Management category. Notice that the higher-capability-level process areas reference the lower-capability-level process areas. Thus the higher-level process areas depend heavily on the lower-level process areas for their implementation. The same type of relationship links Quantitative Project Management to the other Project Management process areas.

Probably the most telling observation is the lack of stand-alone process areas. This view of the model clearly indicates that an organization should pay close attention to its business objectives and ensure that it considers all aspects of the model at the appropriate time.

7.5.2 Relationships between Generic Practices and Process Areas

The references between the generic practices and process areas identify close relationships between those model components, as shown in Table 7-3. A close look reveals generic practices that are similar to those specified in the process areas. The process areas provide some of the "detailed what to do" information for implementing the generic practices. Notice also that each generic practice resides at the same capability level as the related process areas. This correspondence is not a random artifact, but rather was intentionally crafted in this manner to provide the mechanism for staging.

The process areas provide detailed guidance on how to implement the generic practices, which raises some interesting questions about capability and maturity levels. For example, can you be at CL 3 in Configuration Management if GP 2.6 is not met in other process areas? The answer is yes. The generic practices indicate a level of institutionalization separate from the capability level of the process areas. Another interesting question is, Can you tailor an enabling process area? Possibly, but doing so would go against the theory underlying the models. Also, it would certainly make it more difficult to improve other processes by using the generic practices.

7.5.3 Relationships, Complexity, and Common Sense

Clearly, complex relationships exist among the elements of the CMMI models. Many of these stem from the theoretical bases of model-based process improvement, especially those that deal with organizational maturity. Others, like the relationships between the Engineering process areas and the relationships between the generic practice and enabling process areas, have roots in the source models and the work conducted in integrating the various representations.

Remember, however, that the models are guides intended to help development, acquisition, and service teams—not to mystify them. When you encounter a seeming conundrum, you can either consult the process improvement experts or simply make a reasonable decision that solves your immediate problem. Although some occasions will call for special expertise, usually a common-sense, "Gordian knot" approach will provide an answer that meets your needs.

Table 7-3: *Generic Practice References*

Generic Practice	Process Area
GP 2.2 Plan the Process	PP
GP 2.3 Provide Resources	PP
GP 2.4 Assign Responsibility	PP
GP 2.5 Train People	OT, PP
GP 2.6 Manage Configurations	CM
GP 2.7 Identify and Involve Relevant Stakeholders	PP, PMC, IPM
GP 2.8 Monitor and Control the Process	PMC, MA
GP 2.9 Objectively Evaluate Adherence	PPQA
GP 2.10 Review Status with Higher-Level Management	PMC
GP 3.1 Establish a Defined Process	IPM, OPD
GP 3.2 Collect Improvement Information	IPM, OPD, OPF
GP 4.1 Establish Quantitative Objectives for the Process	QPM, OPP
GP 4.2 Stabilize Process Performance	QPM, OPP
GP 5.1 Ensure Continuous Process Improvement	OID
GP 5.2 Correct Root Causes of Problems	CAR

Lewis and Clark Party at Three Forks
Detail from painting by E. S. Paxson,
Missoula County Courthouse, Missoula, Montana

Part III

Using CMMI

On their historic journey of exploration, Meriwether Lewis and William Clark learned from the Nez Perce tribe and from Sacagawea that success in unknown territory often depends on having a knowledgeable guide. The CMMI, while not actually an untamed wilderness, does present a landscape where pitfalls and risks can confront the unwary user. Part III attempts to provide help in selecting the best routes based on your organization's particular continuous improvement needs.

Part III Contents

Chapter 8

Picking a Representation

You must choose . . . but choose wisely.
The Grail Knight, *Indiana Jones and the Last Crusade* (1989)

We choose our joys and sorrows long before we experience them.
Kahlil Gibran, *Sand and Foam* (1926)

Once you have defined the scope of your planned process improvement efforts, your next important decision is to pick an architectural representation: continuous or staged. In Chapter 5, we described the distinguishing features of staged and continuous models, including some basic information about how CMMI provides these two alternative representations in its integrated suite of model products.

Each of the two architectural representations can provide a solid foundation for process improvement. For some people, however, the preference for one representation is deeply rooted and emotionally charged: They may simply mistrust the other representation. For other people, the preference is based on habit and grounded in the source model to which they are accustomed. For most users, this preference will be developed (we hope) through a comprehensive understanding of the benefits (in their organization's specific environment) provided by each representation. Perhaps this choice merits the use of a structured decision-making process and the application of the CMMI process area for Decision Analysis and Resolution. While members of each organization must explore this issue for themselves, this chapter highlights some important issues and considerations in making that decision.

This chapter is arranged so as to start you on the path to making the best decision for your organization. The first two sections address the representations individually and present (for undecided voters or independents) the salient arguments offered by the proponents of each representation. The third section brings these general considerations into the CMMI context.

8.1 Reasons for Liking Staged Models

Staged models have been used successfully and with proven results for many years. This fact heads the list of reasons for using staged models; indeed, it is a powerful argument. Like Washington, D.C., insiders, staged model users can claim, "Real Experience, Real Results." The path from an immature organization to a mature one has been demonstrated repeatedly both in the past with the Software CMM and more recently with CMMI. Use of a staged representation of the model offers the following benefits:

- An ability to manage processes across the organization
- Good communication about process among employees
- Improved accuracy of project estimates
- Improved cost and quality control
- The use of measurable data to guide problem analysis and improvement efforts

These results are made possible and supported by a process infrastructure that provides discipline and motivation for both project and organizational process improvement.

For an organization that is just beginning its journey to greater process maturity, a staged model provides a well-defined and proven path. First the organization's personnel work at process areas that facilitate improved project management (ML 2), then they provide organization-wide process definition (ML 3), and finally they use the standardized process definitions to support quantitative analysis for improving (ML 4) and optimizing (ML 5) project results. By building the staging of the process areas into its architecture, this model offers a clear path for improvement that can be followed without a lot of discussion and debate.

Consider the analogy of a child who is told to clean his room. There are toys everywhere, with nary any floor to be seen. The child just looks at the problem. It seems so overwhelming that he doesn't know where to start. If he is told to pick up the blocks, however, he can sort through the mess and put all of the blocks away. Next, he can be told to pick up the balls and put them away. This process continues until the room is tidy. The approach taken by the staged model is similar, in that the model architects (rather than the model users) decide on the best order for process improvement.

Having a single system for defining process maturity facilitates making improvements over time within an organization. The maturity levels

---

Proven Path, Truth, and Untruth

To speak of a single path to process improvement with a staged model involves both truth and untruth.

The truth is that the maturity levels define plateau stages for process improvement, providing a common general structure for all model users and a predefined ordering of the process areas within a small, finite number of maturity levels. The single path is defined by first requiring the satisfaction of all goals at ML 2, and then continuing stepwise (as appropriate) to the satisfaction of goals that reside at higher maturity levels.

The untruth is any suggestion that within this general structure, all organizations will do things in the same way. For example, the requirement to perform peer reviews on selected work products is part of achieving ML 3. The exact time when this issue is addressed prior to achieving ML 3 and the selection of work products for peer review are both items that can vary greatly among organizations. Thus, when we speak of a single path to improvement with a staged model, understand that we intend to speak the truth, not the untruth.

---

are broadly understood, so that (proponents would argue) there is a single meaning (more or less) regarding what it means for the organization to be at ML 2, for example.[1]

For all of these reasons (and others), staged models have been used by organizations to achieve notable success in support of their efforts related to process improvement.

8.2 Reasons for Liking Continuous Models

The concept of a continuous model for process improvement precedes the development of staged models. The writings of Philip Crosby, for example, define levels for improvement within individual areas.[2] In spite of this heritage, continuous process improvement models have been used less often than staged models, and no systematic data collection related to the business results of continuous model usage has taken place. Nonetheless, there is no shortage of proponents for the continuous approach, especially among systems engineers.

Proponents cite two fundamental reasons for using a continuous (as opposed to a staged) model: freedom and visibility. Unlike a staged model, which provides a single improvement path for all model users, a continuous model offers additional freedom for users, who can select the order for process improvement activities based on their organization's specific business objectives.[3] With a continuous model, individual organizations or organizational groups have the option of defining organizational maturity and an ordering for the process areas which

---

1. By having each process area reside at a specified maturity level and hence at a well-understood position in the path to organizational maturity, the model authors can create more uniform process areas. For example, in a staged model, a process area that is written for ML 2 would differ from a similar process area that is written for ML 3. When appraisals are conducted, the intended scope and application for the process area become very clear, as they are based on the staged level.
2. The five levels of Crosby's Quality Management Maturity Grid are Stage I—Uncertainty; Stage II—Awakening; Stage III—Enlightenment; Stage IV—Wisdom; and Stage V—Certainty. See Crosby, Philip B. *Quality Is Free: The Art of Making Quality Certain.* New York: McGraw-Hill, 1979.
3. Just as a staged model allows for many choices and options, so the wise use of a continuous model requires an understanding of the many inherent ordering relationships between various model elements. As with any freedom, the situation for the user of a continuous model is not "anything goes." In the CMMI continuous representation, for example, the organization needs to reach CL 1 in the Configuration Management process area before it applies the generic practice on configuration management, which resides at CL 2, to any process area. Even without a staging of process areas, CMMI continuous representations have many such ordering constraints. Chapter 7 highlights some of these constraints.

(they may believe) are a better fit for their unique business environment. They may wish to achieve given capability levels for the process areas in an alternative order, rather than accepting the constraints of the "one size fits all" philosophy advocated by proponents of the staged models.

Given that the capability level scale is defined for each process area, an appraisal based on a continuous model may provide increased visibility into process improvement strengths and weaknesses. This greater transparency derives from the way in which the results are reported, rather than the model content. Despite the unflattering portrayal of managers in the cartoon world of "Dilbert," those with more detailed process data can make more informed decisions. For instance, a capability level profile that includes a separate rating for each individual process area could provide greater insight than a single maturity level number.[4] Even a manager who initially may prefer the simplicity of a single number could, in time, develop greater appreciation for the capability profile that only a continuous representation provides. In the end, managers may want both.

By providing more detailed insight that is tailored to the individual business environment, an organization can benefit from the following aspects of the continuous model:

- The complete application of all generic practices in each process area
- A clearer focus on risks that are specific to individual process areas
- A structure that is more immediately compatible with ISO/IEC 15504
- A structure that more easily facilitates the addition of new process areas with minimal effects on the existing model structure

For managers who have used and found benefit in having a single maturity level number, a continuous model can provide the same information. A "staging" is possible with any continuous model,. Fundamentally and simply, a staging comprises a set of rules of the following form: For an organization to be at maturity level x, it must achieve capability level y in process areas $PA_1, PA_2, \ldots, PA_n$.[5] To produce a single

---

4. While a staged model appraisal doesn't normally report a profile, it does provide organizational strengths and weaknesses on a process-area-by-process-area basis.
5. Complex rules are possible. For example, to achieve maturity level x, you must reach capability level y in one set of process areas and capability level z in another set of process areas.

maturity level number, the model need not have a staged architecture; it requires only an algorithm to produce the maturity rating based on a set of staging rules. As described in Section 5.3.3, CMMI includes an equivalent staging for users of the continuous representation.

For organizations that want or need a predefined path for process improvement, a staging mapped onto a continuous model provides the same guidance as a staged model. If some groups support different staging schemes, however, then model users must choose *a* path for process improvement; they will not be given *the* path.

8.3 Reasons for Choosing a CMMI Representation

Based on the considerations cited in the preceding sections for liking either a staged or continuous architectural representation, a decision to favor one or the other would seem to involve almost philosophical musings. On the one hand, all things being equal, having a single number rating score and a proven standard path for process improvement would seem to have many potential benefits. Many organizations would prefer to avoid the "anything goes" approach to process improvement that the continuous representation may seem (incorrectly) to engender. On the other hand, a rating profile may ultimately prove more useful than a single number.

Furthermore, recognizing the realities of different business environments may lead to multiple approaches to process improvement, all of which are equally valid.[6] Most of us would likely prefer to receive the benefits available on both sides. That is, it would be nice to have a relatively small number of choices in process improvement paths (one of which is the most common in any given business environment). Likewise, it would be nice to have clear recognition that one predefined

---

6. Within the U.S. Department of Defense environment, for example, personnel are not far removed from the debates that raged about the programming language Ada. While many claimed that having a single programming language within the Department of Defense offered strong potential benefits, others demurred, citing a need to recognize alternative, equally valid approaches in different kinds of systems. For example, the software in a management information system and the software in a real-time weapon system may be very different. Trade studies of widely varying system types relating to the best choice for a programming language would not rate any one language as always preferable. Sometimes the best place in standardization efforts is the middle ground, somewhere between one (at one extreme) and hundreds (at the other extreme); perhaps three—or seven—approaches would keep everyone happy.

path may not be appropriate for the entire world and all business environments. Finally, it would be nice to have a single number rating for some contexts and a rating profile for other contexts.

Both staged and continuous representations of CMMI certainly hold the promise of at least some benefits. A close examination reveals that the differences between the staged representation and the continuous representation are less pronounced in CMMI v1.2, and the representation choice is less polarized than is the case with the legacy models that are either staged or continuous, but not both.[7] In an effort to ensure that each representation would be just an alternative view of the same base model, both representations are now contained in a single published model version for each constellation, and the process areas in both representations are the same. The primary difference is that the generic goals residing at capability levels 1, 4, and 5 are not needed in the staged representation. The goals (the required items) are also the same. The specific practices (the expected items from individual process areas) are the same. The generic practices are the same for maturity level 2 and 3 generic goals. In an appraisal for maturity level 2, the process areas staged at maturity level 2 use the level 2 generic practices only. In an appraisal for maturity level 3 or higher, all process areas use the level 2 and 3 generic practices.

Because the two representations are so closely aligned, the reasons for preferring one over the other become more practical and less philosophical. Will your organization need less of a training effort with one representation than with the other owing to legacy issues? Is the staging that is integral to the staged architecture and provided in the equivalent staging for the continuous architecture the better one for your business environment? Does management need the detail provided by a capability profile? Questions such as these may not have easy answers, but they can be investigated across all organizational components that seek to develop an integrated process improvement strategy.

Because the two architectural representations in CMMI are not dramatically different, in some ways you cannot make a bad choice: The fundamentals are the same. Perhaps, in time, the use of CMMI will show that two distinct representations are not necessary at all.

---

7. The IPD CMM (the Integrated Product Development model, which served as the third source model for the initial CMMI work) was a hybrid model, as is the FAA-iCMM (the Federal Aviation Administration's model).

Chapter 9

Appraisals
with CMMI

> *Not everything that can be counted counts,*
> *and not everything that counts can be counted.*
> **Albert Einstein** (1879–1955)

> *Good, fast, cheap: Pick any two.*
> Sign in print shop

> *If you don't like something, change it.*
> *If you can't change it, change your attitude.*
> *Don't complain.*
> **Maya Angelou** (1928–)

A comprehensive discussion of process appraisals, their history, the way in which they are addressed in CMMI, rules for ratings, and so forth would require more than the "distilled" presentation offered by this book. The objective of the current chapter is more modest: to briefly introduce the CMMI appraisal process, explain basic appraisal concepts, and discuss some of the issues that an organization may confront when deciding to conduct an appraisal. The appraisal method that is included in the CMMI Product Suite is called the Standard

CMMI Appraisal Method for Process Improvement (SCAMPI[SM]).[1] To help understand why the SCAMPI approach has the features that it does, we begin by reviewing the set of requirements that apply to any appraisal method used with the CMMI model.[2]

9.1 Appraisal Requirements for CMMI

One key part of the CMMI Product Suite is the *Appraisal Requirements for CMMI, Version 1.2* (ARC, V1.2). This technical report comprises 40 "requirements" that provide a mixed set of appraisal method requirements and design constraints. To be "ARC-compliant," an appraisal method must satisfy all (or an appropriate subset) of the 40 ARC requirements. In the jargon of CMMI, an ARC-compliant appraisal method that meets all 40 requirements is called a Class A method. The ARC also defines Class B and Class C method classes, which address only a subset of the 40 ARC requirements. Table 9-1, which was taken from the ARC technical report, outlines some of the salient differences between the method classes.[3]

SCAMPI A is the appraisal method included in the CMMI Product Suite that is ARC-compliant as a Class A method. Just from Table 9-1 alone you already know several features of the SCMAPI A method: Documents and interviews provide evidence to the appraisal team during an appraisal; ratings are generated for the goals in the model, on whether or not they are satisfied; the scope of the appraisal must adequately represent the organization being appraised; an appraisal team of at least four people must be used; and the effort must be led by an authorized lead appraiser.

---

1. SCAMPI is a service mark of Carnegie Mellon University.
2. Of course, in English the word "scampi" denotes large shrimp, or by extension an Italian dish of shrimp served over pasta. While the CMMI appraisal method called SCAMPI has nothing to do with shrimp (certainly not the fishy smell), one may feel the irresistible and perhaps unprofessional urge to develop colorful characterizations of appraisal types. For example, what is shrimp SCAMPI? Answer: an appraisal focused on just one process area. What is chicken SCAMPI? Answer: an appraisal where the lead appraiser comes from inside the organization being appraised. What is pork SCAMPI? Answer: an appraisal conducted by the government. What is squash SCAMPI? Answer: an appraisal conducted by upper management. What is prune SCAMPI? Answer: you tell us! We leave the continuation of this list as an exercise for the reader.
3. CMU/SEI-2006-TR-011, Chapter 3, page 5, Table 1.

Table 9-1: *Requirements of CMMI Appraisal Method Classes*

Requirements	Class A	Class B	Class C
Types of objective evidence gathered	Documents and interviews	Documents and interviews	Documents or interviews
Ratings generated	Goal ratings required	Not allowed	Not allowed
Organizational unit coverage	Required	Not required	Not required
Minimum team size	4	2	1
Appraisal team leader requirements	Lead appraiser	Person trained and experienced	Person trained and experienced

Taking a broader look at the ARC, we see that it comprises seven categories of requirements:

1. *Responsibilities.* Lists the responsibilities of the appraisal sponsor and the leader of the appraisal team.

2. *Appraisal Method Documentation.* Provides items of guidance that should be included in the documentation of a method. As examples, guidance should be provided for identifying the appraisal's purpose, model scope, organizational scope, team member and team leader qualifications, team size, team member and team leader roles, resource estimation, logistics, data collection, findings, data protection, non-attribution, and appraisal records.

3. *Planning and Preparation for the Appraisal.* Identifies a minimum set of appraisal preparation activities and the items needed in an appraisal plan.

4. *Appraisal Data Collection.* Requires the use of two types of objective evidence (conducting interviews and reviewing documentation) for Class A and Class B appraisals, and requires just one of the two types of objective evidence for Class C appraisals.[4]

---

4. Version 1.1 of the ARC also required "administering instruments" such as questionnaires or surveys. That requirement has been dropped in ARC version 1.2.

5. *Data Consolidation and Validation.* Specifies constraints on the way in which an appraisal method provides for the consolidation and validation of the data collected. The topics required include the following:

- Team consensus leading to findings and ratings
- A method for consolidating the data into accurate findings
- A method for validating findings
- A set of criteria for objective evidence to be considered "corroborated" (which entails the use of two different sources and having at least one source reflect work actually being done)[5]
- Sufficiency of data to cover the scope of the appraisal (which entails corroborated objective evidence for each specific or generic practice, such that the extent of the implementation is understood and the data is representative of the organizational unit and the relevant life-cycle phases)
- A mechanism to determine strengths and weaknesses relative to the CMMI model being used
- Feedback of preliminary appraisal findings to the appraisal participants

6. *Rating.* Provides more constraints on what is needed for a capability-level or maturity-level rating. The requirements include the prerequisite of corroborated objective evidence for each practice prior to the rating of goals, a judgment that goals are "satisfied" only when the associated practices are implemented and the aggregate of any weaknesses does not have a significant negative impact on goal achievement, and the basis for a capability-level or maturity-level rating to be the satisfaction of all relevant goals.

7. *Reporting Results.* Requires documentation of the findings and ratings for the appraisal sponsor, and requires a report made to the CMMI Steward (at Carnegie Mellon University).

In three of these seven areas (appraisal data collection, data consolidation and validation, and rating), some of the ARC "requirements" are what might be called "appraisal method design constraints," rather than strict requirements. Performance requirements in this area would focus on issues such as accuracy, repeatability, stability, usefulness, and

---

5. Version 1.1 of the ARC also required that there be data from at least two data-gathering sessions. That requirement has been dropped in ARC version 1.2.

efficiency. The ARC authors included design constraints for one primary reason: to try to ensure the accuracy and repeatability of the appraisal results and ratings. This concern is a carry-over from the Software CMM and the belief that you have to tightly control how appraisals are conducted if you want to get a single maturity rating number—one that could serve as a benchmark and the basis for comparisons across different organizations.[6]

Perhaps we should deepen our understanding of which performance requirements are appropriate for any appraisal method and how to measure against those requirements the results from the application of a method. Then perhaps the ARC might be recast to allow for greater flexibility in developing methods that make different trade-offs between the various quality factors and efficiency (cost).[7]

The Authors' Perspective

How many times have your heard the complaint that CMMI appraisals are too costly? How many times have you heard the complaint that too much attention is devoted to the number ratings?

Organizations that conduct CMMI appraisals are interested especially in three things: the reliability of the appraisal results, the usefulness of the appraisal results for continuous improvement, and the cost of the effort. If the ARC requirements addressed these three areas, then we would have a basis for verifying the extent to which a given appraisal method meets user needs. Currently, however, no ARC requirements address cost efficiency. Furthermore, while ratings to benchmark a process are emphasized in the requirements, insufficient weight is placed on the development of findings useful for process improvement.

(continued)

---

6. After years of experience in this area, your authors continue to be highly skeptical of the validity of using the CMMI model to make maturity-level comparisons across organizations that inherently have many differences. Benchmarking within a single organization and monitoring change over time make sense. Beyond that activity, maturity levels have little value, we believe.

7. This might result also in a shift in the way in which "lead appraisers" compete for business. They could utilize different appraisal methods that offer to an organization increased improvement benefits with decreased expense.

The Authors' Perspective (continued)

Two distinct, but not unrelated, reasons for conducting an appraisal exist: (1) to accurately diagnose internal process problems and areas for process improvement, and (2) to provide a benchmark for process capability or process maturity. These two purposes can pull an organization in opposite directions. The identification of process improvement opportunities requires exposing process weaknesses, whereas the effort made to achieve a benchmark score may encourage the hiding of process weaknesses and the "gaming" of numbers.

In the trade-offs between reliability, accuracy, repeatability, cost, and other factors, we believe, the ARC places too much emphasis on reliability and too little emphasis on cost. This choice is not unrelated to the process improvement versus benchmark tug-of-war. For a benchmark, reliability is a central concern; for process improvement, a somewhat lesser level of reliability may be acceptable if costs are significantly less. The ARC requirements should not be written so that trying to focus on process improvement and reduction of cost means using a "less than full" (i.e., less "good") method.

In the months and years ahead, the CMMI user community needs to collect data on various appraisal methods that make the cost and reliability trade-off in different ways. Eventually, we should have an empirical basis for knowing how much accuracy, reliability, and usefulness of findings were produced at what cost for each proposed appraisal method.

9.2 Standard CMMI Appraisal Method for Process Improvement: Class A

As noted earlier, SCAMPI A (version 1.2) is a Class A method that meets all of the ARC requirements. It was designed to produce benchmark-quality ratings, with multiple uses in mind—namely, internal process improvement and external capability determinations (supplier selection and process monitoring). Its creators wanted to address not only ARC compliance, but also the essential characteristics of accuracy, repeatability, cost- and resource-effectiveness, and meaningfulness of the appraisal results. A central goal of any Class A appraisal is to determine the extent to which the model is implemented.

Of course, if an organization is focused primarily on discovering opportunities for improvement, and so is less interested in a rating, a less-costly Class B or Class C appraisal may be the prudent path. Often such less-costly appraisals are excellent preparation for embarking on the path to a SCAMPI A appraisal.

SCAMPI A can provide a comprehensive look at the process strengths and weaknesses in an organization, which typically leads to planning for process improvement. The ratings that are produced during a SCAMPI A appraisal should reflect the extent to which practices (which support the goals in the CMMI models) are planned and implemented in the organization. To make this determination, the appraisal team collects objective evidence, both at the organization level and within projects, seeking to identify compliance with the CMMI model as well as gaps in compliance.

When planning for an appraisal, the projects (and support groups) that the appraisal team is to review must be identified. The SCAMPI A method provides sampling rules for project (and support group) selection that are intended to lead to a representational look at the organization during the appraisal. For example, both "focus" projects and "non-focus" projects must be identified: Focus projects provide enough evidence to rate every process area in the model, whereas non-focus projects need only provide applicable evidence for a small group of process areas.[8]

During a SCAMPI A appraisal, the organization is encouraged to provide to the appraisal team evidence of its implemented processes, with clear mapping to the goals and practices of the model. Having this information permits the appraisal team to operate in a "verification" mode rather than one of "discovery," making the team's appraisal activity much more efficient and less prone to error.

---

8. Rules in the SCAMPI A method specify how many focus and non-focus projects are required, based on variables such as the number of projects in the organization and the stages of those projects in the development life cycle.

The SCAMPI A method requires the use of three types of *practice implementation indicators*. These "footprints" of an activity or practice provide the basis for verification by the appraisal team:

- *Direct artifacts*—tangible outputs that result from performing a practice (e.g., the plan that results from the practice of establishing a plan)
- *Indirect artifacts*—the consequence of performing a practice, but not its purpose (e.g., the minutes from a planning meeting)
- *Affirmations*—oral or written statements confirming that a practice has been implemented (e.g., an interview with the persons who created or maintain the plan)

A combination of these three indicator types is required during a SCAMPI A appraisal: direct artifacts for each practice in the model, and either indirect artifacts or affirmations for each practice.

A consensus across the entire appraisal team is needed whenever a SCAMPI A appraisal team reaches conclusions about whether practices are implemented across an organizational unit, whether the model goals have been satisfied, and which capability level or maturity level rating is appropriate. Work that leads up to such conclusions may be assigned to smaller subteams for review. Individual strengths and weaknesses that a SCAMPI A appraisal team has identified are aggregated into preliminary findings, which are then presented to the organization for verification, prior to drafting the final findings (and ratings).

Because the CMMI-DEV model is integrated across all development disciplines (systems, hardware, and software), an organization that wishes to obtain ratings (capability or maturity levels) has several options to consider. Specifically, does it want a single rating across the disciplines, or does it want individual ratings for each discipline? While the former permits a stronger discipline to achieve higher ratings than might be warranted through a collective look, a single rating (especially a higher one) may be desired as it would suggest the existence of a well-integrated process structure across the disciplines.

A SCAMPI A appraisal is divided into three phases: (1) plan and prepare for the appraisal; (2) conduct the appraisal; and (3) report the results. Each of these phases includes multiple steps. Phase 1 involves analyzing the organization's business needs and objectives, developing and documenting an appraisal plan, selecting and preparing the appraisal team, obtaining and analyzing the initial practice implementation data, conducting a readiness review, and preparing for the collection on-site of additional objective evidence. Phase 2 involves preparing those who will participate in the on-site appraisal, collecting and examining information obtained both from interviews and from documents,[9] creating records that document practice implementation as well as strengths and weaknesses, verifying the detailed information collected (i.e., looking for gaps and comparing to the CMMI model the practices as implemented in the organization[10]), validating the preliminary findings based on feedback from the organization, and generating the appraisal results (i.e., rating whether the goals in the model are satisfied and determining which capability or maturity levels would be appropriate). Phase 3 involves reporting the appraisal results to the organization and appraisal sponsor, and appropriately packaging and archiving the appraisal assets, including appraisal feedback to the CMMI Steward at Carnegie Mellon.[11]

Any ARC Class A appraisal must be directed by a lead appraiser who has received recognition from an authorizing body to perform that role for the particular appraisal method.[12] In the case of the SCAMPI A method, the lead appraiser must be trained and authorized by the

---

9. A *document* is defined as "a collection of data, regardless of the medium on which it is recorded, that generally has permanence and can be read by humans or machines."

10. The team's characterization regarding how each practice from the model is implemented uses these categories: fully implemented (FI), largely implemented (LI), partially implemented (PI), not implemented (NI), and not yet (NY). The NY characterization is appropriate when the practice in the model applies to a stage in the development life cycle that has not yet been reached.

11. With version 1.2 of the CMMI Product Suite, there is a three-year (maximum) period of validity for SCAMPI Class A appraisals; after that period of time, the appraisal results "expire."

12. Starting with version 1.2 of the CMMI Product Suite, any SCAMPI A appraisal whose results will become part of the public record (such as being announced in a press release) or will be used in a proposal response to U.S. Department of Defense requirements must be headed by a lead appraiser from an external, third-party organization. In other words, an internal lead appraiser is not permitted. Also, before any public-record announcement is issued, the appraisal must first be reviewed and "accepted" (not "confirmed" or "certified") by the CMMI Steward (the SEI at Carnegie Mellon University). Acceptance by the CMMI Steward means that the SCAMPI A method definition was followed and that the Appraisal Disclosure Statement (ADS) meets certain criteria. The goal for turnaround by the SEI Steward is 30 calendar days to provide a response that the appraisal results are either accepted, not accepted, or rejected.

CMMI Steward. To be a lead appraiser, an individual must have relevant discipline experience, knowledge of the CMMI models, and a good understanding of appraisal techniques.[13] The appraisal team leader has the following responsibilities: ensure that the appraisal method is followed; confirm the sponsor's commitment to the appraisal; ensure that the participants are adequately informed about the appraisal plan; ensure that appraisal team members have appropriate experience, knowledge, and skills with regard both to the CMMI model and the appraisal method; verify that all appraisal method requirements have been met; and confirm delivery of the appraisal results to the sponsor.

A significant investment of resources is needed to conduct a cross-disciplinary SCAMPI A appraisal that covers all (or most) of the CMMI model. Data on actual resources used is not always easy to obtain. One set of real data shows that a ML 5 appraisal covering the disciplines of systems, hardware, and software involved about 7000 hours of effort. This number includes time spent by the lead appraiser, the appraisal team, the sponsor, the appraisal coordinator, and the appraisal participants. Of course, the number of hours would vary based on the model scope, the number of disciplines covered, the number of projects interviewed, the size of the appraisal team, the extent to which objective evidence was compiled in advance of the appraisal, and so on.

For organizations that seek to conform to ISO/IEC 15504 (the international standard on process appraisals), SCAMPI A is designed for conformance with that standard.

In summary, here are some key principles to keep in mind when planning any SCAMPI A appraisal:

- Get strong sponsorship from senior management.
- Focus on the business goals for the organization.
- Use the SCAMPI A documented appraisal method.
- Use an appropriate CMMI process reference model.
- Assure confidentiality for interviewees.
- Select and engage a lead appraiser early in the process.

---

13. Recently, there has been an effort by the CMMI Team to better define what the higher maturity levels (ML 4 and ML 5) really mean. To promote greater consistency, there is a new requirement that any lead appraiser conducting a "high maturity" appraisal must have supplemental training and certification related to high-maturity practices.

- Take care when selecting appraisal team members, including taking the following considerations into account: balancing experience in CMMI with the desire to train and expose to CMMI; assuring discipline coverage; matching the organizational scope coverage; and balancing "insiders," who understand the current process well and where to look for evidence, with "outsiders," who bring a fresh set of eyes to the analysis.
- Run an appraisal effort the same way you would run a project.
- Use experienced staff to compile the process implementation indicators.
- Present a process briefing to the appraisal team to (among other things) provide affirmations across the generic practices.
- For high-maturity appraisals, provide to the appraisal team a matrix that maps high-maturity activities both to process areas from the model and to disciplines from the organization.
- Whenever possible, present to the appraisal team process improvement initiatives that are cross-disciplinary in nature.

9.3 The Role of Appraisals in Continuous Improvement

Just as a lean engineering value-stream map can facilitate the identification of waste and highlight opportunities to make gains in process efficiency by reducing that waste, so a CMMI appraisal can provide insight into needed change. The findings from an appraisal might include shortcomings such as these:

- A standard process for something is on the books, but the understanding and use of that process are currently spotty.
- Some programs make important decisions but often fail to capture the assumptions and justifications for those decisions.
- Cost estimates are based on information that in some cases is outdated.
- Efforts in statistical management and control produce potentially useful data, but follow-through is lacking.
- The transfer of information between systems and software is not always well handled.

- Engineering design changes are being used to make architectural changes that have major implications for both cost and schedule.

- Information on employee training and skills is not kept current, and programs are finding it difficult to obtain the skills that they need.

- Some employees believe that making risks known would prove detrimental to their careers.

- The quality group lacks adequate personnel to perform evaluations across all the programs that need them.

- While process improvement efforts have been made in the past, there is little effort to quantify or evaluate the impact of those changes.

When an appraisal is conducted well, each finding can present an opportunity to delve into the root causes of a problem and to make improvements in how the business is conducted. For example, after an appraisal an organization might:

- Conduct a Six Sigma project focusing on how to make better use of statistical control techniques.

- Perform a value-stream mapping exercise focused on how one discipline hands off information to another in an effort to improve that interface.

- Develop a training module to encourage the more widespread use of some successful practice.

Given that the maturity level produced by a CMMI SCAMPI A appraisal can attract large amounts of attention both inside and outside the organization, upper management has a special obligation to keep the focus on improving the business. While getting a maturity level number can be beneficial and help in new business-development efforts, management needs to champion the improvement aspect of a CMMI appraisal as well. After all, the resources expended in conducting an appraisal are such that it would be short-sighted to only care about the number produced by that effort.

CMMI appraisals are an important tool in the continuous improvement toolkit, sometimes highlighting otherwise unnoticed weaknesses and vulnerabilities. A subsequent evaluation of those weaknesses could generate some pointed questions: Can the organization reach its objective of being an employer of choice if current employees are afraid to make risks known? Can financial performance remain good if information used for estimation purposes is outdated? Will customer satisfaction remain high if quality evaluations are skipped?

When a SCAMPI lead appraiser is selected and the team is formed, management needs to make sure everyone knows that it is not just the final number that matters. Whatever maturity-level target may exist, insights into needed improvements to enhance the business are at least as important as a number, if not more so.

The Delphic Sybil
Michaelangelo Buonarotti
Cappella Sistina, Il Vaticano
Scala / Art Resource, NY

Part IV

The Future of CMMI

The historian Herodotus gave an account of King Croesus of Lydia (circa 546 BCE), who asked the Oracle at Delphi to consult the gods, look into the future, and determine whether he should invade Persian territory. The Oracle answered that if he crossed a river, then "Croesus will destroy a great empire." Thinking he would be victorious, Croesus invaded Persia. Unfortunately, it was his own empire that fell and subsequently was destroyed.

Prediction has always been risky. The evolution of thinking about continuous process improvement has been rapid and contentious. In Part IV, the authors don their mystical robes and stare deeply into their scrying crystals in an attempt to predict how CMMI may change in the future.

Part IV Contents

Chapter 10

Evolving CMMI

The rung of a ladder was never meant to rest upon,
but only to hold a man's foot long enough
to enable him to put the other somewhat higher.
Thomas Henry Huxley, *Life and Letters of Thomas Huxley* (1825–1895)

Beware becoming change-averse change agents!
Barry Boehm, SEI Symposium 2000 Keynote Address

When we blindly adopt a religion, a political system,
a literary dogma, we become automatons. We cease to grow.
Anaïs Nin, *The Diaries of Anaïs Nin* (1903–1977)

What lies ahead for Capability Maturity Model Integration (CMMI) and for improvement efforts in general? How will process improvement methods and tools evolve to meet the changing needs of users? Will the concept of constellations—new to version 1.2 of the model—enable CMMI concepts to be more readily applied outside of the engineering disciplines? Will process improvement evolve away from the capability model concept?

Our discussion of (and musings on) such questions in this final chapter may be of greatest interest to those readers who are, in their heart of hearts, architects or system designers. Perhaps as you reflected on our description of the CMMI product suite in earlier chapters you found yourself wondering: "Why did they do it that way?" or "I would have done it differently" or "What *were* they thinking?" Perhaps you are just curious about the use of improvement models in an increasingly agile world. If such questions and issues interest you, read on.

In contrast, if your interest is focused (quite legitimately) on learning about and using the current CMMI products, then you may prefer to make this chapter a "quick read" on your way to the Afterword, which contains our concluding remarks.

10.1 Simplifying the Model

From the very first meetings of the CMMI team, before version 1.0 existed, there have been calls for a simpler model. The original CMMI effort to merge the three source models inevitably required compromises related to the number and scope of the process areas (PAs). The decisions made then and in each revision of the model to date, while certainly thoughtful and deliberate, are not beyond the realm of debate. Are all of the current process areas needed? But beyond size, are there additional simplifications that could or should be made?

One big step toward simplification has already been made: the elimination of the staged and continuous representations as separately published entities. This makes the selection of a model easier for users of version 1.2. After all, the staged and continuous approaches do not represent distinct ways to make improvements as much as different ways of presenting appraisal results.

What steps are possible in the future? There has been discussion about the complexity of the model architecture, and the concept of generic practices (GPs) is a favorite target for critics of the model. As described in Section 10.3, a primary reason for GP bashing may be a lack of understanding about how they work. Of course, the GPs might also be a good place to try to simplify the model—albeit while working within the concept rather than outside it. Rewriting or rethinking GPs to reduce their number and clarify their meaning is certainly a possibility. The following sections provide for reflection and discussion of some ideas and questions on the future of CMMI.

10.2 A Domain-Independent CMMI Model

There are always creative people who see opportunities to apply existing tools in new ways. Often, this sort of extension leads to changes in the tools as new stakeholder views are considered. CMMI can be a powerful vehicle for process improvement. In particular, it can be effective in identifying and mitigating risk in engineering, acquisition, and service organizations. If we wish to expand the domains to which CMMI may be applied, then changes in the overall CMMI concept and in the architecture of the model may be needed. In this section we look at one way to both simplify the model and use it in a much broader set of process domains.

With the advent of CMMI, and its inclusion of multiple engineering disciplines within a single architectural framework, the world of engineering process models was supposed to become more unified. The original CMMI architecture team spent a good deal of time trying to identify a hierarchy of process areas that would be represented in any domain. The constellation process built on this experience by defining the CMMI Model Foundation. The common elements in the CMF need to be interpreted and amplified for each domain in which they are applied.

Several members of the CMMI Team have long advocated a simpler, more streamlined approach to CMMI. One idea is to produce a model consisting of only generic practices and the process areas that "enable" or support them.[1] Written in a conceptual and extensible manner, those components would define a model that could apply to any process—engineering, acquisition, service, or otherwise. There would be a template for defining domain-specific and organization-specific target processes. Process capability levels would be measured by the implementation of generic practices. Maturity levels would be based on the staging of the enabling process areas in the same way as the current CMMI equivalent staging.

As an example, suppose that a printing company wanted to apply this domain-independent CMMI (DI-CMMI) to its processes. It would first

---

1. For example, a process area for configuration management that supports the Configuration Management generic practice at CL 2.

need to establish its "core discipline" processes—perhaps layout, printing, finishing, and delivery—according to the template provided with the DI-CMMI. Once these processes were defined, the company could begin improvement with the level 2 generic practices and their enabling process areas.

Although the domain-independent model would be similar to the existing CMMI models, its lack of an orientation toward a particular constellation would provide several broad benefits:

- It could act as a process improvement model for a much wider range of enterprises, such as banking, consulting services, light industry, government, and retail; such applications already have been suggested by countries with the need to institute various industrial and governmental processes in their emerging economies.

- It could provide a layperson's view of continuous improvement that could be taught in undergraduate management and business curricula.

- Because of its lean structure, it would not require large development teams or a complex support infrastructure to apply it to additional disciplines.

A DI-CMMI may also have some drawbacks. For instance, it is not clear that the language in the model could be suitably simplified so as to apply across all disciplines. Some question might arise as to the comparability of level ratings, given the variation in the organization-specific processes.[2] Of course, training and appraisal materials would be needed that were as simple and clear as the model language, and most likely there would still be trainers and appraisers available to "guide" its use.

This approach could support an improvement community working to develop agile techniques, and would open up additional opportunities for improvement experts to expand their practices—possibly working in some specialty disciplines where they had additional interests. It could be used throughout the enterprise, from the CEO's processes down to the processes found at the lowest level of the organizational hierarchy. It could also energize a number of communities that to date have been lukewarm to the current models because they are "too engi-

---

2. As noted earlier, we are not big fans of using CMMI ratings to compare organizations that have significant differences.

neering oriented." Finally, it would enable process engineering to evolve with the successful practices of the various domains.

10.3 Collection of Issues for Beyond Version 2.1

The CMMI sponsors held a number of workshops in 2007 with the goal of capturing ideas from users about the evolution of CMMI. Our readers should keep an eye out for similar workshops in the future. So far these sessions have brought to light some common themes that may be useful in evolving CMMI.[3]

10.3.1 Misunderstanding of Current Model Concepts

Not surprisingly, the workshops brought forth many more comments about appraisals and the appraisal process than about the model content and architecture. However, some of the appraisal issues may be based on a misunderstanding of the model. This was particularly true of the GP concept. It was striking how many people—including some folks who should—didn't "get" GPs. There was also wide misunderstanding of capability levels and maturity levels, especially by more senior management. Correcting this state of affairs by making adjustments to the GPs and to how levels are characterized may be one of the goals defined in evolving CMMI.

One contributor to this issue may be the language used in the model itself. To be both precise in its content and generic in applicability, the model is written using words that—while carefully chosen—may be difficult to understand for average readers. Just as requirements and operational concepts should be written in terms that users and customers understand, so it may be necessary to find new ways to describe the model's components and requirements. In the future we hope to see considerable innovation in this area.

10.3.2 Project and Program Process Improvement

Another issue that arose was the request for more project-related process improvement. CMMI, which relies on the notion of a "road to maturity," is based on the concept of an organizational institutionaliza-

---

3. In this section, we highlight just some of the ideas currently under discussion.

tion of common processes. This assumption is perfectly reasonable for an organization that has several units that do roughly the same thing. However, that environment is rarer now than it was in the 1970s and 1980s when the original CMM concepts were defined.

Consider the current way in which systems with software are developed. Big, complex systems are usually developed by a team of large, multidisciplinary corporations that represent the result of a decade of mergers, buyouts, and other culture and process mixers. Pieces used to build the system are bought as commercial items from smaller companies, custom-developed by suppliers, obtained from open-source libraries, created internally from scratch, or are vestigial or legacy components. Every such project deals with different issues. What is the "corporate organization" in that scenario?

At the same time, software development and other engineering tasks are being driven by the need for agility in response to rapidly changing and emergent requirements and the expectations of early value to the customer. Agile approaches usually include mechanisms for improvement on a cycle-by-cycle basis, where the effects of new process components—whether good or bad—can be determined within weeks (rather than months and years). Unfortunately, most of the more traditional development and improvement approaches, while not totally inconsistent with agile thinking, are generally not supportive and, in some cases, are actually antagonistic.

Are there ways in which organizational maturity and multi-organizational maturity might be better integrated into the continuous improvement paradigm? Can future versions of CMMI (or improvement in general) move toward a more flexible approach that could work for programs and projects without forcing the assumption of artificial organizational constructs? Could process improvement be somehow coupled to acquisition or development milestones, perhaps requiring evidence of continuous improvement before moving to the next phase? This issue is somewhat addressed in the Boehm/IBM rational anchor-point milestones, where evidence must be presented as to the feasibility of the project or program, including the ability to meet the cost and schedule targets based on the results of the prior phase.[4] To address this concern within the current models requires reconsideration of some of the core

---

4. Boehm, B., and R. Turner, *Balancing Agility and Discipline: A Guide for the Perplexed,* Addison-Wesley, Boston, 2005 (Appendix D).

concepts of CMMI and so will be painful and expensive—but then so is childbirth, and the result could be just as exciting to watch grow and mature.[5]

10.3.3 Process Performance

One of the continuing conundrums within the improvement community is whether the existing models and appraisal approaches give sufficient consideration to whether a process is working effectively, which is a central facet of lean engineering improvement techniques. Is the CMMI infrastructure supporting better end results or just more consistent and predictable results? The model authors will state unequivocally that the whole rationale for CMMI is to support better end results by improving organizational performance. Nevertheless, questions come from a large number of doubters, including some in the U.S. Department of Defense (DoD), who believe that the models (perhaps because of the hype about maturity level numbers) are more means of marketing and competitive comparison than serious improvement initiatives. In support of this view they point to a lack of statistical evidence that higher-level organizations actually perform better than lower-level ones on their contracts. The paucity of data leads to the question of how the models and appraisal methods can evolve to better accomplish the prime directive of continuously making improvements.

10.3.4 Improvement Scope

Probably the most interesting—and frustrating—issue is the question of model scope. On the one hand, there is strong support for simplifying the model. On the other hand, there is equally strong support for extending the model to more disciplines. On the surface, these perspectives seem to imply exactly opposite requirements. The constellation concept was intended to bridge this gap by providing a means to create new but highly compatible models. Since this concept was implemented, however, some sponsors and users have pushed back a good deal. While the original requirements for CMMI specifically included the need for extensibility into other disciplines and subject areas, some

---

5. While he was working on revisions to this chapter, Rich welcomed his first grandchild, Ian Fred Kadera, into this world. Dennis is expecting his first grandchild (a girl) in 2008. We all continue to be fascinated with how quickly a baby changes and changes those around him.

believe that constellations hearken back to the proliferation of CMMs, the elimination of which was a central goal of the CMMI project from the beginning. It may be that a radical change in the way the model is defined (e.g., something similar to the domain-independent proposal) could simplify model application while leading to a broader scope for CMMI. Only time and politics will determine which, if either, of these constituencies is satisfied.

10.3.5 Steering Group and Sponsorship

Now it's time to venture into really dangerous territory: Who should control CMMI? Currently, the product suite is controlled primarily by the U.S. defense industry. The decision authority for any changes to the model or to the disciplines is concentrated within three groups: the National Defense Industrial Association (NDIA), the acquisition organization of the U.S. Department of Defense (OUSD AT&L), and a federally funded research and development corporation (the SEI), which is sponsored by the DoD. While non-defense industry is represented as part of this initiative, members of the Steering group—which is co-chaired by NDIA and DoD—serve as the "deciders." And the deciders are focused on DoD and its large suppliers, and on maintaining their investments in the current models. This is not bad per se, but there is a question whether this power structure is good for the long-term health of the model. Although it does provide much-needed stability, it also makes it very difficult to make significant changes and may bias the direction of CMMI evolution.

Several voices have called for the defense community to turn the model over to a more domain-neutral organization. It is not clear exactly how this handoff would be accomplished, given that the intellectual property belongs to Carnegie Mellon University; while provided ostensibly free of charge, CMMI remains a considerable asset to the University. Standards organizations such as ISO have been mentioned as a possible CMMI home. One benefit of this could be a broadening of interest in CMMI across a more diverse range of disciplines and industries. On the downside, however, standards organizations are governed by notoriously slow processes when developing or updating standards, typically they charge for copies of standards, and they are sometimes innovation averse. Although some CMMI practitioners may not like everything about the current CMMI products, decisions can be made relatively quickly under the current system when there is the need to do so. Other ideas for governance include pursuing an open-source approach, which means that the models would be able to change rapidly given that the changes are "tested and approved" by the source control team. Of course, that begs a new question: What will be the membership of the source control team?

Obviously, this very thorny and highly political issue will not be resolved quickly; just embarking on the discussion would require goodwill and trust in many places. Nevertheless, as the model finds proponents in more countries and more industries, this conversation may become more vibrant and change could come. We hope this subject is pursued in an open and positive manner, engaging all the stakeholders in the discussion and giving support to the best ideas and rationales that are presented.

10.4 A Final Note on CMMI Evolution

The ideas presented in this chapter are no more than seeds of possibilities. How CMMI actually evolves should be driven by you—that is, by the user community. At the end of the day, if CMMI isn't useful to organizations like yours, it won't be applied; it will stagnate, wither, and disappear into the graveyard of lost management tools du jour. Conversely, if CMMI remains responsive to your needs by changing to better serve organizations like yours, it will be a vital and beneficial tool for a long period of time.

Widespread acceptance and adoption require the user community to actively participate in CMMI evolution. There are a number of ways you can join this movement:

- Attend conferences, workshops, and courses to learn more about CMMI and to provide feedback to the sponsors.
- Submit change requests to the CMMI Stewart (SEI).
- Join organizations that are sponsors, and actively lobby for your positions on CMMI issues.
- Participate in a CMMI working group such as the interpretive guidance project or a model extension development team.
- Have your organization (or your industry association) join the CMMI Steering Group.

The more users who become involved, each of whom brings his or her diverse needs and viewpoints to the table, the better CMMI will be. And the better CMMI is, the easier it will be for integrated, continuous process improvement to benefit more and more organizations throughout the world. It really is up to you.

Afterword

Before putting this volume aside, consider the incredible amounts of creativity, imagination, composition, frustration, genius, and plain hard work that have led to the current CMMI Product Suite. Think about the millions of hours of effort spent as hundreds of people applied CMMI models and methods to improve thousands of organizations around the world. We continue to marvel at CMMI's impact on technical and business enterprises, and we can only guess at what the future holds.

After a decade of development and use, the level of intellectual energy around the content, structure, and application of CMMI continues unabated. There is and always will be tension between the desire to improve, change, and grow, and the desire for stability and an avoidance of moving targets. Because both change and stability are fundamental to continuous process improvement, this tension is particularly strong within the CMMI community. The CMMI Product Suite must have sufficient stability so that an investment in improvement is not undercut by radical and pervasive changes to the models. At the same time, CMMI must change to incorporate new knowledge, proven experience, and the continuous creativity of those who practice and preach process improvement. As every proponent of continuous improvement knows, change focused on making improvements never ends. Surely this axiom applies to process improvement models just as much as it does to engineering development processes.

Throughout this book, we have tried to distill our experiences in responding to the need for an integrated approach to continuous process improvement. We hope that we have provided an accessible view into CMMI so that you can make more informed decisions about applying this model in your organization.

Chapter 1 began with a quote from W. Edwards Deming, which proves as useful at this juncture as it did for our opening act: "It is not necessary to change. Survival is not mandatory." As you have survived your reading of this book, please let us know whether it has helped you on your path to improvement. Like processes and process improvement models, books about these topics can be improved. We look forward to hearing from you and using your suggestions in future editions.

Three Selections from "A Process Improvement Songbook"

by Richard Turner, *with apologies to musicians everywhere*[1]

1. CMMI (Norwegian Wood)

> *I once had a plan, or should I say, it once had me…*
> *It showed me the way, never ask why, CMMI.*
>
> *The plan said the task was too long for the schedule we had,*
> *But Brooks said to add to the team would really be bad.*
>
> *I re-scoped the plan, biding my time, fighting a whine.*
> *We worked through phase two, the client then said, put this to bed.*
>
> *She told us long lead-time was late and we sighed all around.*
> *We told them quickly that our team was still within bounds.*
> *And within a month we were in synch, back from the brink.*
> *So, we smelled of rose, you may ask why, CMMI.*

2. The Team That's Level One (The House of the Rising Sun)

> *There is a team at Level One,*
> *Chaotic work they do.*
> *It's been the ruin of many a career,*
> *And Watts, I know it's true.*
>
> *They started work without a plan,*
> *Too short of schedule and cash.*
> *They struggled on against all odds,*
> *But ended up in the trash.*
>
> *Executives were fuming,*
> *About the defects released.*
> *The customers were lawyering up,*
> *Convinced that they'd been fleeced.*
>
> *The courtroom was all empty,*
> *It never came to trial.*
> *The settlement was a small country's worth,*
> *And all the lawyers just smiled.*

---

1. This is just a sampling of the inane songs about process improvement written and performed, with little coaxing required, by Richard Turner. The Songbook of which they are a part, as well as Turner's performances of them, may or may not be available for download from the Addison-Wesley Professional Web site, a decision that the publisher was still trying to avoid as we went to press.

Now Mothers tell your children,
Not to do what they have done.
To spend their lives in futile work,
On the team, that's Level One.

3. I Can't Help Peer Reviewing You (I Can't Help Falling in Love with You)

Fagan says, it take's a team I know;
But I can't help peer reviewing you.

Shall I stay, break the process flow?
If I can't help peer reviewing you.

Those process police,
Audit you and me,
Darling we'll at least
Attempt a waiver, please.

Take my role, take my defects, too.
For I can't help peer reviewing you.

Appendix A

Summary of CMMI Models

CMMI Model Foundation

The 16 process areas in the CMF are listed here:

- Organizational Process Definition +IPPD (OPD+IPPD)
- Organizational Process Focus (OPF)
- Organizational Process Performance (OPP)
- Organizational Innovation and Deployment (OID)
- Organizational Training (OT)
- Project Planning (PP)
- Project Monitoring and Control (PMC)
- Integrated Project Management +IPPD (IPM+IPPD)
- Quantitative Project Management (QPM)
- Risk Management (RSKM)
- Requirements Management (REQM)
- Configuration Management (CM)
- Process and Product Quality Assurance (PPQA)

- Measurement and Analysis (MA)
- Decision Analysis and Resolution (DAR)
- Causal Analysis and Resolution (CAR)

The generic goals and practices are also included in the foundation and are listed following the process areas. The process areas are listed by category in the following sections.

PROCESS MANAGEMENT

Organizational Process Definition +IPPD

Establish and maintain a usable set of organizational process assets and work environment standards.

IPPD Addition

For IPPD, Organizational Process Definition +IPPD also covers the establishment of organizational rules and guidelines that enable conducting work using integrated teams.

A set of organizational process assets is established and maintained. SG 1

Establish and maintain the organization's set of standard processes. SP 1.1

Establish and maintain descriptions of the life-cycle models approved for use in the organization. SP 1.2

Establish and maintain the tailoring criteria and guidelines for the organization's set of standard processes. SP 1.3

Establish and maintain the organization's measurement repository. SP 1.4

Establish and maintain the organization's process asset library. SP 1.5

Establish and maintain work environment standards. SP 1.6

IPPD Addition

Organizational rules and guidelines, which govern the operation of integrated teams, are provided. SG 2

Establish and maintain empowerment mechanisms to enable timely decision making. SP 2.1

Establish and maintain organizational rules and guidelines for structuring and forming integrated teams. SP 2.2

Establish and maintain organizational guidelines to help team members balance their team and home organization responsibilities. SP 2.2

Organizational Process Focus

Plan, implement, and deploy organizational process improvements based on a thorough understanding of the current strengths and weaknesses of the organization's processes and process assets.

Strengths, weaknesses, and improvement opportunities for the organization's processes are identified periodically and as needed. SG 1

Establish and maintain the description of the process needs and objectives for the organization. SP 1.1

Appraise the organization's processes periodically and as needed to maintain an understanding of their strengths and weaknesses. SP 1.2

Identify improvements to the organization's processes and process assets. SP 1.3

Process actions that address improvements to the organization's processes and process assets are planned and implemented. SG 2

Establish and maintain process action plans to address improvements to the organization's processes and process assets. SP 2.1

Implement process action plans. SP 2.2

The organizational process assets are deployed across the organization and process-related experiences are incorporated into the organizational process assets. SG 3

Deploy organizational process assets across the organization. SP 3.1

Deploy the organization's set of standard processes to projects at their startup and deploy changes to them as appropriate throughout the life of each project. SP 3.2

Monitor the implementation of the organization's set of standard processes and use of process assets on all projects. SP 3.3

Incorporate process-related work products, measures, and improvement information derived from planning and performing the process into the organizational process assets. SP 3.4

Organizational Process Performance

Establish and maintain a quantitative understanding of the performance of the organization's set of standard processes in support of quality and process-performance objectives, and to provide the process-performance data, baselines, and models to quantitatively manage the organization's projects.

Baselines and models, which characterize the expected process performance of the organization's set of standard processes, are established and maintained. SG 1

Select the processes or subprocesses in the organization's set of standard processes that are to be included in the organization's process performance analyses. SP 1.1

Establish and maintain definitions of the measures that are to be included in the organization's process-performance analyses. SP 1.2

Establish and maintain quantitative objectives for quality and process performance for the organization. SP 1.3

Establish and maintain the organization's process-performance baselines. SP 1.4

Establish and maintain the process-performance models for the organization's set of standard processes. SP 1.5

Organizational Innovation and Deployment

Select and deploy incremental and innovative improvements that measurably improve the organization's processes and technologies. The improvements support the organization's quality and process-performance objectives as derived from the organization's business objectives.

Process and technology improvements, which contribute to meeting quality and process-performance objectives, are selected. SG 1

Collect and analyze process- and technology-improvement proposals. SP 1.1

Identify and analyze innovative improvements that could increase the organization's quality and process performance. SP 1.2

Pilot process and technology improvements to select which ones to implement. SP 1.3

Select process and technology improvements for deployment across the organization. SP 1.4

Measurable improvements to the organization's processes and technologies are continually and systematically deployed. SG 2

Establish and maintain the plans for deploying the selected process and technology improvements. SP 2.1

Manage the deployment of the selected process and technology improvements. SP 2.2

Measure the effects of the deployed process and technology improvements. SP 2.3

Organizational Training

Develop the skills and knowledge of people so they can perform their roles effectively and efficiently.

A training capability, which supports the organization's management and technical roles, is established and maintained. SG 1

Establish and maintain the strategic training needs of the organization. SP 1.1

Determine which training needs are the responsibility of the organization and which will be left to the individual project or support group. SP 1.2

Establish and maintain an organizational training tactical plan. SP 1.3

Establish and maintain training capability to address organizational training needs. SP 1.4

Training necessary for individuals to perform their roles effectively is provided. SG 2

Deliver the training following the organizational training tactical plan. SP 2.1

Establish and maintain records of the organizational training. SP 2.2

Assess the effectiveness of the organization's training program. SP 2.3

PROJECT MANAGEMENT

Project Planning

Establish and maintain plans that define project activities.

Estimates of project planning parameters are established and maintained. SG 1

Establish a top-level work breakdown structure (WBS) to estimate the scope of the project. SP 1.1

Establish and maintain estimates of the attributes of the work products and tasks. SP 1.2

Define the project life-cycle phases on which to scope the planning effort. SP 1.3

Estimate the project effort and cost for the work products and tasks based on estimation rationale. SP 1.4

A project plan is established and maintained as the basis for managing the project. SG 2

Establish and maintain the project's budget and schedule. SP 2.1

Identify and analyze project risks. SP 2.2

Plan for the management of project data. SP 2.3

Plan for necessary resources to perform the project. SP 2.4

Plan for knowledge and skills needed to perform the project. SP 2.5

Plan the involvement of identified stakeholders. SP 2.6

Establish and maintain the overall project plan content. SP 2.7

Commitments to the project plan are established and maintained. SG 3

Review all plans that affect the project to understand project commitments. SP 3.1

Reconcile the project plan to reflect available and estimated resources. SP 3.2

Obtain commitment from relevant stakeholders responsible for performing and supporting plan execution. SP 3.3

Project Monitoring and Control

Provide an understanding of the project's progress so that appropriate corrective actions can be taken when the project's performance deviates significantly from the plan.

Actual performance and progress of the project are monitored against the project plan. SG 1

Monitor the actual values of the project planning parameters against the project plan. SP 1.1

Monitor commitments against those identified in the project plan. SP 1.2

Monitor risks against those identified in the project plan. SP 1.3

Monitor the management of project data against the project plan. SP 1.4

Monitor stakeholder involvement against the project plan. SP 1.5

Periodically review the project's progress, performance, and issues. SP 1.6

Review the accomplishments and results of the project at selected project milestones. SP 1.7

Corrective actions are managed to closure when the project's performance or results deviate significantly from the plan. SG 2

Collect and analyze the issues and determine the corrective actions necessary to address the issues. SP 2.1

Take corrective action on identified issues. SP 2.2

Manage corrective actions to closure. SP 2.3

Integrated Project Management +IPPD

Establish and manage the project and the involvement of the relevant stakeholders according to an integrated and defined process that is tailored from the organization's set of standard processes. It also covers the establishment of a shared vision for the project and the establishment of integrated teams that will carry out the objectives of the project.

The project is conducted using a defined process that is tailored from the organization's set of standard processes. SG 1

Establish and maintain the project's defined process from project startup through the life of the project. SP 1.1

Use the organizational process assets and measurement repository for estimating and planning the project's activities. SP 1.2

Establish and maintain the project's work environment based on the organization's work environment standards. SP 1.3

Integrate the project plan and the other plans that affect the project to describe the project's defined process. SP 1.4

Manage the project using the project plan, the other plans that affect the project, and the project's defined process. SP 1.5

Contribute work products, measures, and documented experiences to the organizational process assets. SP 1.6

Coordination and collaboration of the project with relevant stakeholders is conducted. SG 2

Manage the involvement of the relevant stakeholders in the project. SP 2.1

Participate with relevant stakeholders to identify, negotiate, and track critical dependencies. SP 2.2

Resolve issues with relevant stakeholders. SP 2.3

The project is managed using IPPD principles. SG 3

Establish and maintain a shared vision for the project. SP 3.1

Establish and maintain the integrated team structure for the project. SP 3.2

Allocate requirements, responsibilities, tasks, and interfaces to teams in the integrated team structure. SP 3.3

Establish and maintain integrated teams in the structure. SP 3.4

Ensure collaboration among interfacing teams. SP 3.5

Risk Management

Identify potential problems before they occur so that risk-handling activities can be planned and invoked as needed across the life of the product or project to mitigate adverse impacts on achieving objectives.

Preparation for risk management is conducted. SG 1

Determine risk sources and categories. SP 1.1

Define the parameters used to analyze and categorize risks, and the parameters used to control the risk management effort. SP 1.2

Establish and maintain the strategy to be used for risk management. SP 1.3

Risks are identified and analyzed to determine their relative importance. SG 2

Identify and document the risks. SP 2.1

Evaluate and categorize each identified risk using the defined risk categories and parameters, and determine its relative priority. SP 2.2

Risks are handled and mitigated, where appropriate, to reduce adverse impacts on achieving objectives. SG 3

Develop a risk mitigation plan for the most important risks to the project as defined by the risk management strategy. SP 3.1

Monitor the status of each risk periodically and implement the risk mitigation plan as appropriate. SP 3.2

Quantitative Project Management

Quantitatively manage the project's defined process to achieve the project's established quality and process-performance objectives.

The project is quantitatively managed using quality and process-performance objectives. SG 1

Establish and maintain the project's quality and process-performance objectives. SP 1.1

Select the subprocesses that compose the project's defined process based on historical stability and capability data. SP 1.2

Select the subprocesses of the project's defined process that will be statistically managed. SP 1.3

Monitor the project to determine whether the project's objectives for quality and process performance will be satisfied, and identify corrective action as appropriate. SP 1.4

The performance of selected subprocesses within the project's defined process is statistically managed. SG 2

Select the measures and analytic techniques to be used in statistically managing the selected subprocesses. SP 2.1

Establish and maintain an understanding of the variation of the selected subprocesses using the selected measures and analytic techniques. SP 2.2

Monitor the performance of the selected subprocesses to determine their capability to satisfy their quality and process-performance objectives, and identify corrective action as necessary. SP 2.3

Record statistical and quality management data in the organization's measurement repository. SP 2.4

ENGINEERING

Requirements Management

Manage the requirements of the project's products and product components and identify inconsistencies between those requirements and the project's plans and work products.

Requirements are managed and inconsistencies with project plans and work products are identified. SG 1

Develop an understanding with the requirements providers on the meaning of the requirements. SP 1.1

Obtain commitment to the requirements from the project participants. SP 1.2

Manage changes to the requirements as they evolve during the project. SP 1.3

Maintain bidirectional traceability among the requirements and work products. SP 1.4

Identify inconsistencies between the project plans and work products and the requirements. SP 1.5

SUPPORT

Configuration Management

Establish and maintain the integrity of work products using configuration identification, configuration control, configuration status accounting, and configuration audits.

Baselines of identified work products are established. SG 1

Identify the configuration items, components, and related work products that will be placed under configuration management. SP 1.1

Establish and maintain a configuration management and change management system for controlling work products. SP 1.2

Create or release baselines for internal use and for delivery to the customer. SP 1.3

Changes to the work products under configuration management are tracked and controlled. SG 2

Track change requests for the configuration items. SP 2.1

Control changes to the configuration items. SP 2.2

Integrity of baselines is established and maintained. SG 3

Establish and maintain records describing configuration items. SP 3.1

Perform configuration audits to maintain integrity of the configuration baselines. SP 3.2

Process and Product Quality Assurance

Provide staff and management with objective insight into processes and associated work products.

Adherence of the performed process and associated work products and services to applicable process descriptions, standards, and procedures is objectively evaluated. SG 1

Objectively evaluate the designated performed processes against the applicable process descriptions, standards, and procedures. SP 1.1

Objectively evaluate the designated work products and services against the applicable process descriptions, standards, and procedures. SP 1.2

Noncompliance issues are objectively tracked and communicated, and resolution is ensured. SG 2

Communicate quality issues and ensure resolution of noncompliance issues with the staff and managers. SP 2.1

Establish and maintain records of the quality assurance activities. SP 2.2

Measurement and Analysis

Develop and sustain a measurement capability that is used to support management information needs.

Measurement objectives and activities are aligned with identified information needs and objectives. SG 1

Establish and maintain measurement objectives that are derived from identified information needs and objectives. SP 1.1

Specify measures to address the measurement objectives. SP 1.2

Specify how measurement data will be obtained and stored. SP 1.3

Specify how measurement data will be analyzed and reported. SP 1.4

Measurement results, which address identified information needs and objectives, are provided. SG 2

Obtain specified measurement data. SP 2.1

Analyze and interpret measurement data. SP 2.2

Manage and store measurement data, measurement specifications, and analysis results. SP 2.3

Report results of measurement and analysis activities to all relevant stakeholders. SP 2.4

Decision Analysis and Resolution

Analyze possible decisions using a formal evaluation process that evaluates identified alternatives against established criteria.

Decisions are based on an evaluation of alternatives using established criteria. SG 1

Establish and maintain guidelines to determine which issues are subject to a formal evaluation process. SP 1.1

Establish and maintain the criteria for evaluating alternatives, and the relative ranking of these criteria. SP 1.2

Identify alternative solutions to address issues. SP 1.3

Select the evaluation methods. SP 1.4

Evaluate alternative solutions using the established criteria and methods. SP 1.5

Select solutions from the alternatives based on the evaluation criteria. SP 1.6

Causal Analysis and Resolution

Identify causes of defects and other problems and take action to prevent them from occurring in the future.

Root causes of defects and other problems are systematically determined. SG 1

Select the defects and other problems for analysis. SP 1.1

Perform causal analysis of selected defects and other problems and propose actions to address them. SP 1.2

Root causes of defects and other problems are systematically addressed to prevent their future occurrence. SG 2

Implement the selected action proposals that were developed in causal analysis. SP 2.1

Evaluate the effect of changes on process performance. SP 2.2

Record causal analysis and resolution data for use across the project and organization. SP 2.3

Generic Goals and Generic Practices

The process supports and enables achievement of the specific goals of the process area by transforming identifiable input work products to produce identifiable output work products. GG 1

Perform the specific practices of the process area to develop work products and provide services to achieve the specific goals of the process area. GP 1.1

The process is institutionalized as a managed process. GG 2

Establish and maintain an organizational policy for planning and performing the process. GP 2.1

Establish and maintain the plan for performing the process. GP 2.2

Provide adequate resources for performing the process, developing the work products, and providing the services of the process. GP 2.3

Assign responsibility and authority for performing the process, developing the work products, and providing the services of the process. GP 2.4

Train the people performing or supporting the process as needed. GP 2.5

Place designated work products of the process under appropriate levels of control. GP 2.6

Identify and involve the relevant stakeholders of the process as planned. GP 2.7

Monitor and control the process against the plan for performing the process and take appropriate corrective action. GP 2.8

Objectively evaluate adherence of the process against its process description, standards, and procedures, and address noncompliance. GP 2.9

Review the activities, status, and results of the process with higher level management and resolve issues. GP 2.10

The process is institutionalized as a defined process. GG 3

Establish and maintain the description of a defined process. GP 3.1

Collect work products, measures, measurement results, and improvement information derived from planning and performing the process to support the future use and improvement of the organization's processes and process assets. GP 3.2

The process is institutionalized as a quantitatively managed process. GG 4

Establish and maintain quantitative objectives for the process, which address quality and process performance, based on customer needs and business objectives. GP 4.1

Stabilize the performance of one or more subprocesses to determine the ability of the process to achieve the established quantitative quality and process-performance objectives. GP 4.2

The process is institutionalized as an optimizing process. GG 5

Ensure continuous improvement of the process in fulfilling the relevant business objectives of the organization. GP 5.1

Identify and correct the root causes of defects and other problems in the process. GP 5.2

Development Constellation

The six process areas in the Development constellation are listed here:

- Requirements Development (RD)
- Technical Solution (TS)
- Product Integration (PI)
- Validation (VAL)
- Verification (VER)
- Supplier Agreement Management (SAM)

ENGINEERING

Requirements Development

Produce and analyze customer, product, and product component requirements.

Stakeholder needs, expectations, constraints, and interfaces are collected and translated into customer requirements. SG 1

Elicit stakeholder needs, expectations, constraints, and interfaces for all phases of the product life cycle. SP 1.1

Transform stakeholder needs, expectations, constraints, and interfaces into customer requirements. SP 1.2

Customer requirements are refined and elaborated to develop product and product component requirements. SG 2

Establish and maintain product and product-component requirements, which are based on the customer requirements. SP 2.1

Allocate the requirements for each product component. SP 2.2

Identify interface requirements. SP 2.3

The requirements are analyzed and validated, and a definition of required functionality is developed. SG 3

Establish and maintain operational concepts and associated scenarios. SP 3.1

Establish and maintain a definition of required functionality. SP 3.2

Analyze requirements to ensure that they are necessary and sufficient. SP 3.3

Analyze requirements to balance stakeholder needs and constraints. SP 3.4

Validate requirements to ensure the resulting product will perform as intended in the user's environment. SP 3.5

Technical Solution

Design, develop, and implement solutions to requirements. Solutions, designs, and implementations encompass products, product components, and product-related life-cycle processes either singly or in combinations as appropriate.

Product or product component solutions are selected from alternative solutions. SG 1

Develop alternative solutions and selection criteria. SP 1.1

Select the product component solutions that best satisfy the criteria established. SP 1.2

Product or product component designs are developed. SG 2

Develop a design for the product or product component. SP 2.1

Establish and maintain a technical data package. SP 2.2

Design product component interfaces using established criteria. SP 2.3

Evaluate whether the product components should be developed, purchased, or reused based on established criteria. SP 2.4

Product components, and associated support documentation, are implemented from their designs. SG 3

Implement the designs of the product components. SP 3.1

Develop and maintain the end-use documentation. SP 3.2

Product Integration

Assemble the product from the product components, ensure that the product, as integrated, functions properly, and deliver the product.

Preparation for product integration is conducted. SG 1

Determine the product component integration sequence. SP 1.1

Establish and maintain the environment needed to support the integration of the product components. SP 1.2

Establish and maintain procedures and criteria for integration of the product components. SP 1.3

The product component interfaces, both internal and external, are compatible. SG 2

Review interface descriptions for coverage and completeness. SP 2.1

Manage internal and external interface definitions, designs, and changes for products and product components. SP 2.2

Verified product components are assembled and the integrated, verified, and validated product is delivered. SG 3

Confirm, prior to assembly, that each product component required to assemble the product has been properly identified, functions according to its description, and that the product component interfaces comply with the interface descriptions. SP 3.1

Assemble product components according to the product integration sequence and available procedures. SP 3.2

Evaluate assembled product components for interface compatibility. SP 3.3

Package the assembled product or product component and deliver it to the appropriate customer. SP 3.4

Verification

Ensure that selected work products meet their specified requirements.

Preparation for verification is conducted. SG 1

Select the work products to be verified and the verification methods that will be used for each. SP 1.1

Establish and maintain the environment needed to support verification. SP 1.2

Establish and maintain verification procedures and criteria plans for the selected work products. SP 1.3

Peer reviews are performed on selected work products. SG 2

Prepare for peer reviews of selected work products. SP 2.1

Conduct peer reviews on selected work products and identify issues resulting from the peer review. SP 2.2

Analyze data about preparation, conduct, and results of the peer reviews. SP 2.3

Selected work products are verified against their specified requirements. SG 3

Perform verification on the selected work products. SP 3.1

Analyze the results of all verification activities. SP 3.2

Validation

Demonstrate that a product or product component fulfills its intended use when placed in its intended environment.

Preparation for validation is conducted. SG 1

Select products and product components to be validated and the validation methods that will be used for each. SP 1.1

Establish and maintain the environment needed to support validation. SP 1.2

Establish and maintain procedures and criteria for validation. SP 1.3

The product or product components are validated to ensure that they are suitable for use in their intended operating environment. SG 2

Perform validation on the selected products and product components. SP 2.1

Analyze the results of the validation activities. SP 2.2

PROJECT MANAGEMENT

Supplier Agreement Management

Manage the acquisition of products from suppliers.

Agreements with the suppliers are established and maintained. SG 1

Determine the type of acquisition for each product or product component to be acquired. SP 1.1

Select suppliers based on an evaluation of their ability to meet the specified requirements and established criteria. SP 1.2

Establish and maintain formal agreements with the supplier. SP 1.3

Agreements with the suppliers are satisfied by both the project and the supplier. SG 2

Perform activities with the supplier as specified in the supplier agreement. SP 2.1

Select, monitor, and analyze processes used by the supplier. SP 2.2

Select and evaluate work products from the supplier of custom-made products. SP 2.3

Ensure that the supplier agreement is satisfied before accepting the acquired product. SP 2.4

Transition the acquired products from the supplier to the project. SP 2.5

Acquisition Constellation

The six process areas in the Acquisition constellation are listed here:

- Agreement Management (AM)
- Acquisition Requirements Development (ARD)
- Acquisition Technical Management (ATS)
- Acquisition Validation (AVAL)
- Acquisition Verification (AVER)
- Solicitation and Supplier Agreement Development (SSAD)

AGREEMENT MANAGEMENT

Ensure that the supplier and the acquirer perform according to the terms of the supplier agreement.

The terms of the supplier agreement are met by both the acquirer and the supplier. SG 1

Perform activities with the supplier as specified in the supplier agreement. SP 1.1

Select, monitor, and analyze supplier processes. SP 1.2

Ensure that the supplier agreement is satisfied before accepting the acquired product. SP 1.3

Manage invoices submitted by the supplier. SP 1.4

ACQUISITION REQUIREMENTS DEVELOPMENT

Develop and analyze customer and contractual requirements.

Stakeholder needs, expectations, constraints, and interfaces are collected and translated into customer requirements. SG 1

Elicit stakeholder needs, expectations, constraints, and interfaces for all phases of the product life cycle. SP 1.1

Transform stakeholder needs, expectations, constraints, and interfaces into prioritized customer requirements. SP 1.2

Customer requirements are refined and elaborated into contractual requirements. SG 2

> Establish and maintain contractual requirements that are based on customer requirements. SP 2.1

> Allocate contractual requirements to supplier deliverables. SP 2.2

Requirements are analyzed and validated. SG 3

> Establish and maintain operational concepts and associated scenarios. SP 3.1

> Analyze requirements to ensure they are necessary and sufficient. SP 3.2

> Analyze requirements to balance stakeholder needs and constraints. SP 3.3

> Validate requirements to ensure the resulting product performs as intended in the user's environment. SP 3.4

ACQUISITION TECHNICAL MANAGEMENT

Evaluate the supplier's technical solution and manage selected interfaces of that solution.

Supplier technical solutions are evaluated to confirm that contractual requirements continue to be met. SG 1

> Select supplier technical solutions to be analyzed and analysis methods to be used. SP 1.1

> Analyze selected supplier technical solutions. SP 1.2

> Conduct technical reviews with the supplier as defined in the supplier agreement. SP 1.3

Selected interfaces are managed. SG 2

> Select interfaces to manage. SP 2.1

> Manage selected interfaces. SP 2.2

ACQUISITION VALIDATION

Demonstrate that an acquired product or service fulfills its intended use when placed in its intended environment.

Preparation for validation is conducted. SG 1

> Select products and product components to be validated and the validation methods to be used. SP 1.1

Establish and maintain the environment needed to support validation. SP 1.2

Establish and maintain procedures and criteria for validation. SP 1.3

Selected products and product components are validated to ensure they are suitable for use in their intended operating environment. SG 2

Perform validation on selected products and product components. SP 2.1

Analyze results of validation activities. SP 2.2

ACQUISITION VERIFICATION

Assure that selected work products meet their specified requirements.

Preparation for verification is conducted. SG 1

Select work products to be verified and verification methods to be used. SP 1.1

Establish and maintain the environment needed to support verification. SP 1.2

Establish and maintain verification procedures and criteria for the selected work products. SP 1.3

Peer reviews are performed on selected work products. SG 2

Prepare for peer reviews of selected work products. SP 2.1

Conduct peer reviews of selected work products and identify issues resulting from these reviews. SP 2.2

Analyze data about the preparation, conduct, and results of the peer reviews. SP 2.3

Selected work products are verified against their specified requirements. SG 3

Perform verification on selected work products. SP 3.1

Analyze results of all verification activities. SP 3.2

SOLICITATION AND SUPPLIER AGREEMENT DEVELOPMENT

Prepare a solicitation package, select one or more suppliers to deliver the product or service, and establish and maintain the supplier agreement.

Preparation for solicitation and supplier agreement development is performed. SG 1

Identify and qualify potential suppliers. SP 1.1

Establish and maintain a solicitation package that includes the requirements and proposal evaluation criteria. SP 1.2

Review the solicitation package with stakeholders to ensure that the approach is realistic and can reasonably lead to the acquisition of a usable product. SP 1.3

Distribute the solicitation package to potential suppliers for their response and maintain the package throughout the solicitation. SP 1.4

Suppliers are selected using a formal evaluation. SG 2

Evaluate proposed solutions according to documented proposal evaluation criteria. SP 2.1

Establish and maintain negotiation plans to use in completing a supplier agreement. SP 2.2

Select suppliers based on an evaluation of their ability to meet specified requirements and established criteria. SP 2.3

Supplier agreements are established and maintained. SG 3

Establish and maintain a mutual understanding of the agreement with selected suppliers and end users based on acquisition needs and the suppliers' proposed approaches. SP 3.1

Establish and maintain the supplier agreement. SP 3.2

Services Constellation

The nine process areas in the draft version of the Services constellation are listed here:

- Organizational Service Management (OSM; addition)
- Capacity and Availability Management (CAM)
- Service Continuity (SCON; addition)
- Requirements Management +SVC (REQM+SVC)
- Problem Management (PM)
- Incident and Request Management (IRM)

- Service Delivery (SD)
- Service System Development (SSD; addition)
- Service Transition (ST)

PROCESS MANAGEMENT

Organizational Service Management (Addition)

Establish and maintain standard services that ensure the satisfaction of the organization's customer base.

Long-term customer satisfaction data is gathered and analyzed. SG 1

Gather data about customer satisfaction that informs the organization about alignment between customer needs and standard services. SP 1.1

Analyze customer satisfaction data to identify opportunities to improve, delete, or add standard services. SP 1.2

Translate the needs of the organization's set of customers into decisions about services to be developed. SP 1.3

A set of organizational services is established and maintained. SG 2

Establish and maintain the organization's set of standard services and service levels. SP 2.1

Establish and maintain descriptions of the services that are approved for use in the organization. SP 2.2

Establish and maintain the tailoring criteria and guidelines for the organization's set of standard services. SP 2.3

Establish and maintain the organization's standard service repository. SP 2.4

PROJECT MANAGEMENT

Capacity and Availability Management

Plan and monitor the effective provision of resources to support service requirements.

Preparation for capacity and availability management is conducted.
SG 1

Establish and maintain the strategy for capacity and availability management. SP 1.1

Select the measures and analytic techniques to be used in managing the capacity and availability of the service system. SP 1.2

Establish and maintain baselines and models to support capacity and availability management. SP 1.3

Capacity and availability are analyzed and monitored to manage resources and demand. SG 2

Analyze and monitor the use of resources and services on an ongoing basis. SP 2.1

Monitor availability against agreed targets. SP 2.2

Report capacity and availability management data to relevant stakeholders. SP 2.3

Service Continuity (Addition)

Establish and maintain contingency plans for continuity of agreed services during and following any significant disruption of normal operations.

The current functions, resources, and work products of the organization on which services depend are identified, documented, and prioritized. SG 1

Identify the essential functions that the organization must perform to ensure service continuity. SP 1.1

Identify internal and external dependencies and interdependencies to ensure service continuity. SP 1.2

Identify organization vital records and databases for service continuity. SP 1.3

The Service Continuity Plan (SCP) is established and maintained. SG 2

Develop a Service Continuity Plan that, if executed, would enable an organization to resume performing its agreed-to services. SP 2.1

Document the tests that measure and validate the effectiveness of the Service Continuity Plan. SP 2.2

Develop training materials and delivery methods to train for the Service Continuity Plan. SP 2.3

Maintain the Service Continuity Plan based on changing environment and service needs. SP 2.4

The effectiveness of the Service Continuity Plan is validated. SG 3

Conduct Service Continuity Plan execution training and evaluate effectiveness of this training. SP 3.1

Execute Service Continuity Plan tests. SP 3.2

Evaluate results from the tests of the Service Continuity Plan and identify areas for corrective action. SP 3.3

ENGINEERING

Requirements Management +SVC

Manage the requirements of the project's products and product components, and identify inconsistencies between those requirements and the project's plans and work products. Establish and maintain written agreements between service providers and customers on service requirements and service levels.

Requirements are managed and inconsistencies with project plans and work products are identified. SG 1

Develop an understanding with the requirements providers on the meaning of the requirements. SP 1.1

Obtain commitment to the requirements from the project participants. SP 1.2

Manage changes to the requirements as they evolve during the project. SP 1.3

Maintain bidirectional traceability among the requirements and work products. SP 1.4

Identify inconsistencies between the project plans and work products and the requirements. SP 1.5

Service requirements agreements are established and maintained. SG 2

Analyze existing agreements and service data against requested service requirements. SP 2.1

Establish and maintain the service requirements agreement. SP 2.2

SUPPORT

Problem Management

Prevent incidents from recurring by identifying and addressing underlying causes of incidents.

Preparation for problem management is conducted. SG 1

Establish and maintain the strategy to be used for problem management. SP 1.1

Establish and maintain a problem management system for recording problem information. SP 1.2

Problems are identified and addressed. SG 2

Identify and record problems. SP 2.1

Analyze, review, and address problems. SP 2.2

Monitor the resolution of problems and escalate if necessary. SP 2.3

Communicate the status of problems and validate the resolution of problems. SP 2.4

Service Establishment and Delivery

INCIDENT AND REQUEST MANAGEMENT

Ensure the timely resolution of requests for service and incidents that occur during service delivery.

Preparation for incident and request management is conducted. SG 1

Establish and maintain the strategy to be used for incident and request management. SP 1.1

Establish and maintain an incident and request management system for recording incident and request information. SP 1.2

Incidents and requests are identified and managed. SG 2

Identify and record incidents and requests. SP 2.1

Analyze, review, and manage incidents and requests. SP 2.2

Monitor the resolution of incidents and requests and escalate if necessary. SP 2.3

Communicate the status of incidents and requests and validate the resolution of incidents and requests with the submitters of incidents and requests. SP 2.4

SERVICE DELIVERY

Deliver services in accordance with service agreements.

Preparation for service delivery is conducted. SG 1

Establish and maintain a service delivery operational plan. SP 1.1

Prepare the appropriate service systems for delivering the services in accordance with the service delivery operational plan. SP 1.2

Services are delivered in accordance with their service agreements. SG 2

Confirm that the appropriate service systems are operational in their intended operating environments. SP 2.1

Acquire service system consumables to enable delivery of services in accordance with their service agreements. SP 2.2

Deliver services by operating service systems in accordance with the service delivery operational plan. SP 2.3

Monitor service delivery for expected performance and customer satisfaction, and take appropriate corrective actions. SP 2.4

Maintain the service systems to ensure continuation of service delivery. SP 2.5

SERVICE SYSTEM DEVELOPMENT (ADDITION)

Analyze, design, develop, integrate, and test service systems to satisfy existing or anticipated service agreements.

Required service functionality is determined through development, analysis, elaboration, and validation of stakeholder needs, expectations, and constraints. SG 1

Collect and transform stakeholder needs, expectations, constraints, and interfaces into stakeholder requirements. SP 1.1

Refine and elaborate stakeholder requirements to develop service and service system requirements. SP 1.2

Develop and define the required service system functionality based upon analyzed and validated requirements. SP 1.3

Solutions to service requirements are selected, designed, implemented, and integrated. SG 2

Select service system component solutions from alternative solutions. SP 2.1

Develop designs for service system components. SP 2.2

Manage internal and external interface definitions, designs, and changes for services and service system components. SP 2.3

Implement the design of service system components and document their intended use, operation, and maintenance. SP 2.4

Assemble and integrate implemented service system components into verifiable configurations. SP 2.5

Selected service system components and services are verified and validated to ensure correct operational service delivery. SG 3

Establish and maintain an approach and an environment for verification and validation. SP 3.1

Perform peer reviews on selected service system components. SP 3.2

Verify selected service system components against their specified requirements. SP 3.3

Validate service delivery capabilities to ensure that they will be suitable for use in the intended operating environment and will meet stakeholder expectations. SP 3.4

SERVICE TRANSITION

Deploy new or significantly changed service systems while managing their effect on ongoing service delivery.

Preparation for service system transition into the operational environment is conducted. SG 1

Ensure the operational functionality and compatibility of the service system in the current operating environment. SP 1.1

Establish and maintain a transition plan for deployment of the service system. SP 1.2

Review plans with stakeholders and obtain commitment to the plan. SP 1.3

The service system is deployed to the operational environment. SG 2

Establish and maintain a baseline. SP 2.1

Package, distribute, integrate, and install service system components within the operational environment. SP 2.2

Test the capability to deliver services against operational scenarios within the operational environment. SP 2.3

Prepare users and service provider personnel for changes in services and in the planned service availability. SP 2.4

Assess the impacts to stakeholders and delivered services after deploying the service system and take appropriate corrective action. SP 2.5

The service system is retired according to plan from the operational environment. SG 3

Plan for the removal of the service system from the operational environment. SP 3.1

As required, maintain service system work products for future retrieval. SP 3.2

Remove the service system from the operational environment. SP 3.3

Appendix B

References

Bate, Roger, Dorothy Kuhn, Curt Wells, et al. *A Systems Engineering Capability Maturity Model, Version 1.1* (CMU/SEI-95-MM-003). Pittsburgh: Software Engineering Institute, Carnegie Mellon University, November 1995.

Boehm, Barry, and Richard Turner, *Balancing Agility and Discipline: A Guide for the Perplexed*. Boston: Addison-Wesley, 2003.

Britcher, Robert. *The Limits of Software.* Reading, MA: Addison-Wesley, 1999.

Carr, M., and W. N. Crowder. *Continuous Appraisal Method (CAM): A New Paradigm for Benchmarking Process Maturity.* Proceedings of the Tenth Annual International Symposium of the International Council on Systems Engineering (INCOSE), Minneapolis, MN, July 16–20, 2000.

Chrissis, Mary Beth, Mike Konrad, and Sandy Shrum. *CMMI: Guidelines for Process Integration and Product Improvement* (2nd ed.). Boston: Addison-Wesley, 2006.

Clouse, Aaron, and R. Shaw. *An Integrated Product Development Process Case Study.* Proceedings of the Sixth Annual International Symposium of the International Council on Systems Engineering (INCOSE), Boston, MA, July 7–11, 1996, vol. I, pp. 541–546.

Crosby, P. B. *Quality Is Free: The Art of Making Quality Certain.* New York: McGraw-Hill, 1979.

Curtis, Bill, Bill Hefley, and Sally Miller. *People Capability Maturity Model (P-CMM) Version 2.0* (CMU/SEI-2001-MM-001). Pittsburgh: Software Engineering Institute, Carnegie Mellon University, September 2001.

Deming, W. Edwards. *Out of the Crisis.* Cambridge, MA: MIT Center for Advanced Engineering, 1986.

Department of Defense. *DOD Directive 5000.1: The Defense Acquisition System.* Washington, DC: Department of Defense, May 2003.

Department of Defense. *DODI 5000.2: Defense Acquisition Guidebook.* Washington, DC: Department of Defense, December 2004.

Department of Defense. *DOD Guide to Integrated Product and Process Development (Version 1.0).* Washington, DC: Office of the Under Secretary of Defense (Acquisition and Technology), February 5, 1996. http://www.acq.osd.mil/te/survey/table_of_contents.html.

Dunaway, D., and S. Masters. *CMM-Based Appraisal for Internal Process Improvement (CBA IPI): Method Description* (CMU/SEI-96-TR-007). Pittsburgh: Software Engineering Institute, Carnegie Mellon University, April 1996.

EIA Interim Standard, Systems Engineering Capability. EIA/IS 731 (Part 1: Model, EIA/IS 731-1, V 1.0; Part 2: Appraisal Method, EIA/IS 731-2, V 1.0), 1999.

Eisner, H. *Essentials of Project and Systems Engineering Management.* New York: Wiley Interscience, 1997.

Federal Aviation Administration—Integrated Capability Maturity Model (FAA-iCMM), Version 2.0: An Integrated Capability Maturity Model for Enterprise-wide Improvement. Washington, DC: Federal Aviation Administration, September 2001.

Ferguson, Jack, Jack Cooper, Michael Falat, et al. *Software Acquisition Capability Maturity Model Version 1.01* (CMU/SEI-96-TR-020). Pittsburgh: Software Engineering Institute, Carnegie Mellon University, December 1996.

Freeman, D., M. Hinkey, and J. Martak. *Integrated Engineering Process Covering All Engineering Disciplines.* Software Engineering Process Group Conference (SEPG '99), March 8–11, 1999, Atlanta, GA. Pittsburgh: Software Engineering Institute, Carnegie Mellon University, 1999.

Garcia, Suzanne, and Richard Turner. *CMMI Survival Guide: Just Enough Process Improvement.* Boston: Addison-Wesley, 2006.

George, Michael L. *Lean Six Sigma: Combining Six Sigma Quality with Lean Speed.* New York: McGraw-Hill, 2002.

Goldenson, D., and J. Herbsleb. *After the Appraisal: A Systematic Survey of Process Improvement, Its Benefits, and Factors That Influence Success* (CMU/SEI-95-TR-009). Pittsburgh: Software Engineering Institute, Carnegie Mellon University, 1995.

Hayes, Will, and David Zubrow. *Moving On Up: Data and Experience Doing CMM-Based Process Improvement* (CMU/SEI-95-TR-008). Pittsburgh: Software Engineering Institute, Carnegie Mellon University, 1995.

Herbsleb, James, David Zubrow, Dennis Goldenson, Will Hayes, and Mark Paulk. "Software Quality and the Capability Maturity Model." *Communications of the ACM,* 40, June 1977, pp. 30–40.

Humphrey, Watts S. *Managing the Software Process.* Reading, MA: Addison-Wesley, 1989.

Humphrey, Watts S. *Winning with Software.* Boston: Addison-Wesley, 2002.

Ibrahim, Linda. *Using an Integrated Capability Maturity Model—The FAA Experience.* Proceedings of the Tenth Annual International Symposium of the International Council on Systems Engineering (INCOSE), Minneapolis, MN, July 16–20, 2000, pp. 643–648.

Ibrahim, Rosalind, and I. Hirmanpour. *The Subject Matter of Process Improvement: A Topic and Reference Source for Software Engineering Educators and Trainers* (CMU/SEI-95-TR-003). Pittsburgh: Software Engineering Institute, Carnegie Mellon University, May 1995.

IEEE Standard Glossary of Software Engineering Terminology [IEEE Standard 610.12-1990 (R2002)]. New York: Institute of Electrical and Electronics Engineers, 2002.

International Organization for Standardization. *ISO 9000:2005, Quality Management Systems: Fundamentals and Vocabulary.* New York: International Organization for Standardization, 2005.

International Organization for Standardization and International Electrotechnical Commission. *Systems and Software Engineering: Measurement*

Process (ISO/IEC 15939:2007). Geneva, Switzerland: International Organization for Standardization/International Electrotechnical Commission, 2007.

International Organization for Standardization and International Electrotechnical Commission. *Systems and Software Engineering: Software Life Cycle Processes (ISO/IEC 12207:2008)*. Geneva, Switzerland: International Organization for Standardization/International Electrotechnical Commission, 2008.

International Organization for Standardization and International Electrotechnical Commission. *Systems and Software Engineering: System Life Cycle Processes (ISO/IEC 15288:2008)*. Geneva, Switzerland: International Organization for Standardization/International Electrotechnical Commission, 2008.

Juran, J. M. *Juran on Planning for Quality*. New York: MacMillan, 1988.

Masters, Steve, Sandi Behrens, Judah Mogilensky, and Charlie Ryan. *SCAMPI Lead Appraiser[SM] Body of Knowledge (SLA BOK)* (CMU/SEI-2007-TR-019). Pittsburgh: Software Engineering Institute, Carnegie Mellon University, October 2007.

Masters, S., and C. Bothwell. *CMM Appraisal Framework* (CMU/SEI-95-TR-001). Pittsburgh: Software Engineering Institute, Carnegie Mellon University, February 1995.

Paulk, Mark C. "The Evolution of the SEI's Capability Maturity Model for Software." *Software Process—Improvement and Practice,* 1995, pp. 3–15.

Paulk, Mark C., Bill Curtis, Mary Beth Chrissis, and Charles V. Weber. *Capability Maturity Model[SM] for Software, Version 1.1* (CMU/SEI-93-TR-24; ESC-TR-93-177). Pittsburgh: Software Engineering Institute, Carnegie Mellon University, February 1993.

Pyzdek, Thomas. *The Six Sigma Handbook: A Complete Guide for Green Belts, Black Belts, and Managers at All Levels*. New York: McGraw-Hill, 2003.

Radice, R. A., J. T. Harding, P. E. Munnis, and R. W. Phillips. "A Programming Process Study." *IBM Systems Journal,* 38(2–3), 1999, pp. 297–307.

Radice, R. A., and R. W. Phillips. *Software Engineering, an Industrial Approach, Vol. 1*. Englewood Cliffs, NJ: Prentice Hall, 1988.

Siviy, Jeannine M., M. Lynn Penn, and Robert W. Stoddard. *CMMI and Six Sigma: Partners in Process Improvement.* Boston: Addison-Wesley, 2007.

Software Engineering Institute. *Appraisal Requirements for CMMI, Version 1.2 (ARC, V1.2)* (CMU/SEI-2006-TR-011). Pittsburgh: Software Engineering Institute, Carnegie Mellon University, August 2006.

Software Engineering Institute. *Introduction to the Architecture of the CMMI Framework* (CMU/SEI-2007-TN-009). Pittsburgh: Software Engineering Institute, Carnegie Mellon University, July 2007.

Software Engineering Institute. *Standard CMMI Appraisal Method for Process Improvement (SCAMPI) A, Version 1.2: Method Definition Document* (CMU/SEI-2006-HB-002). Pittsburgh: Software Engineering Institute, Carnegie Mellon University, July 2006.

Systems Engineering Capability Assessment Model, Version 1.50. International Council on Systems Engineering, June 1996.

Womack, James P., and Daniel Jones. *Lean Thinking.* New York: Simon and Schuster, 1996.

SEI Figure Credit List

Figure 7-2 © 2006 by Carnegie Mellon University. Introduction to CMMI V1.2-Module 9-082506, page 18

Figure 7-3 © 2006 by Carnegie Mellon University. Introduction to CMMI V1.2-Module 9-082506, page 11

Figure 7-4 ©2006 by Carnegie Mellon University. Introduction to CMMI V1.2-Module 10-080906, page 23

Figure 7-5 © 2006 by Carnegie Mellon University. Introduction to CMMI V1.2-Module 9-082506, page 34

Figure 7-6 © 2006 by Carnegie Mellon University. Introduction to CMMI V1.2-Module 9-082506, page 40

Figure 7-8 © 2006 by Carnegie Mellon University. Introduction to CMMI V1.2-Module 6-082506, page 9

Figure 7-9 © 2006 by Carnegie Mellon University. Introduction to CMMI V1.2-Module 6-082506, page 20

Figure 7-10 © 2006 by Carnegie Mellon University. Introduction to CMMI V1.2-Module 9-082506, page 25

Figure 7-11 © 2006 by Carnegie Mellon University. Introduction to CMMI V1.2-Module 11-082506, page 20

Figure 7-12 © 2006 by Carnegie Mellon University. Introduction to CMMI V1.2-Module 10-082506, page 29

Figure 7-13 © 2006 by Carnegie Mellon University. Introduction to CMMI V1.2-Module 6-082506, page 26

Figure 7-14 © 2006 by Carnegie Mellon University. Introduction to CMMI V1.2-Module 5-082506, page 36

Figure 7-15 © 2006 by Carnegie Mellon University. Introduction to CMMI V1.2-Module 7-082506, page 9

Figure 7-16 © 2006 by Carnegie Mellon University. Introduction to CMMI V1.2-Module 7-082506, page 16

Figure 7-17 © 2006 by Carnegie Mellon University. Introduction to CMMI V1.2-Module 7-082506, page 23

Figure 7-18 © 2006 by Carnegie Mellon University. Introduction to CMMI V1.2-Module 7-082506, page 31

Figure 7-19 © 2006 by Carnegie Mellon University. Introduction to CMMI V1.2-Module 7-082506, page 38

Figure 7-20 © 2006 by Carnegie Mellon University. Introduction to CMMI V1.2-Module 5-082506, page 22

Figure 7-21 © 2006 by Carnegie Mellon University. Introduction to CMMI V1.2-Module 8-082506, page 9

Index

A

Learn More About the Carnegie Mellon® Software Engineering Institute (SEI)

The 2007 SEI Annual Report is available at *www.sei.cmu.edu/annual-report*. It describes the accomplishments of the SEI during fiscal year 2007 (October 1, 2006, through September 30, 2007). The report profiles people at the SEI whose contributions are shaping the future of software engineering and transferring methods and techniques to the broad software community.

The SEI Guide to Products and Services is available at *www.sei.cmu.edu/publications/guide.pdf*. It is a complete catalog of all the SEI's tools and methods, services, courses, conferences, credentials, books, and opportunities to collaborate with the SEI on research.

Software Engineering Institute
Carnegie Mellon

Achieve "Faster, Better, Cheaper" Mission Success Using CMMI and Six Sigma Together

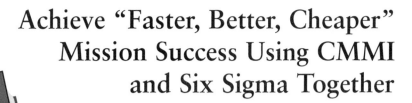

Jeannine M. Siviy | M. Lynn Penn | Robert W. Stoddard

ISBN: 978-0-321-51608-4

"In this book, I have found answers to key questions and misconceptions about the relationship between Six Sigma and the Capability Maturity Model Integration [CMMI] . . .. Among my key takeaways is that the relationship between Six Sigma and CMMI exemplifies one of the principles of S4/IEE: CMMI provides process infrastructure that is needed to support a successful Six Sigma strategy."

—Forrest W. Breyfogle III, CEO, Smarter Solutions, Inc.

"Finally, a book that bridges the software and hardware process tool set. To date, there have been hardware and software engineers who for one reason or another have not communicated their process methods. And so, myths formed that convinced the hardware community that CMMI was only for software and likewise convinced the software community that Six Sigma was only for hardware. It is both refreshing and thought-provoking to dispel these myths."

—Jack Ferguson, Manager, SEI Appraisal Program, Software Engineering Institute

Also available at safari.informit.com

The SEI Series in Software Engineering

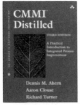
ISBN 0-321-46108-8

ISBN 0-321-22876-6

ISBN 0-321-11886-3

ISBN 0-201-73723-X

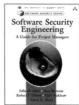
ISBN 0-321-50917-X

ISBN 0-321-15495-9

ISBN 0-321-17935-8

ISBN 0-321-27967-0

ISBN 0-201-70372-6

ISBN 0-201-70482-X

ISBN 0-201-70332-7

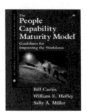
ISBN 0-201-60445-0

ISBN 0-201-60444-2

ISBN 0-321-42277-5

ISBN 0-201-52577-1

ISBN 0-201-25592-8

ISBN 0-321-47717-0

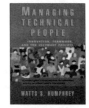
ISBN 0-201-54597-7

ISBN 0-201-54809-7

ISBN 0-321-30549-3

ISBN 0-201-18095-2

ISBN 0-201-54610-8

ISBN 0-201-47719-X

ISBN 0-321-34962-8

ISBN 0-201-77639-1

ISBN 0-201-73-1134

ISBN 0-201-61626-2

ISBN 0-201-70454-4

ISBN 0-201-73409-5

ISBN 0-201-85-4805

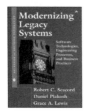
ISBN 0-321-11884-7

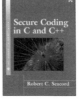
ISBN 0-321-33572-4

ISBN 0-321-51608-7

ISBN 0-201-70312-2

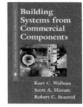
ISBN 0-201-70-0646

ISBN 0-201-17782-X

Please see our web site at informit.com/seiseries for more information on these titles.

ESSENTIAL GUIDES TO CMMI

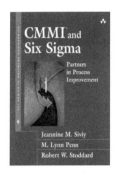

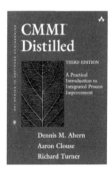

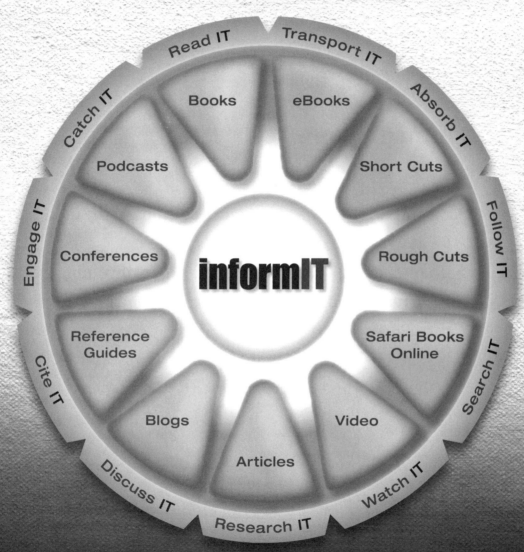

Learn IT at InformIT

Go Beyond the Book

informIT

- Read IT
  - Books
- Transport IT
  - eBooks
- Absorb IT
  - Short Cuts
- Catch IT
  - Podcasts
- Follow IT
  - Rough Cuts
- Engage IT
  - Conferences
- Cite IT
  - Reference Guides
- Search IT
  - Safari Books Online
- Discuss IT
  - Blogs
- Watch IT
  - Video
  - Articles
- Research IT

11 WAYS TO LEARN IT at **www.informIT.com/learn**

The online portal of the information technology
publishing imprints of Pearson Education

Register Your Book

at informit.com/register

You may be eligible to receive:

- Advance notice of forthcoming editions of the book
- Related book recommendations
- Chapter excerpts and supplements of forthcoming titles
- Information about special contests and promotions throughout the year
- Notices and reminders about author appearances, tradeshows, and online chats with special guests

Contact us

If you are interested in writing a book or reviewing manuscripts prior to publication, please write to us at:

Editorial Department
Addison-Wesley Professional
75 Arlington Street, Suite 300
Boston, MA 02116 USA
Email: AWPro@aw.com

Visit us on the Web: informit.com/aw